Issues and Problems

in Contemporary

Educational Administration

Issues and Problems in Contemporary Educational Administration

KEITH GOLDHAMMER   **JOHN E. SUTTLE**

WILLIAM D. ALDRIDGE   **GERALD L. BECKER**

THE CENTER FOR THE ADVANCED STUDY OF
EDUCATIONAL ADMINISTRATION

UNIVERSITY OF OREGON
Eugene, Oregon
1967

The Center for the Advanced Study of Educational Administration at the University of Oregon is a national research and development center which was established under the provisions of the Cooperative Research Program of the United States Office of Education. The research reported herein was performed pursuant to a grant from the Bureau of Research, Office of Education, U. S. Department of Health, Education, and Welfare. No federal funds were used in the publication of this report.

Printed in the United States of America
at the University of Oregon Press, Eugene, Oregon

Designed and edited by Joanne M. Kitchel

The text of this book is set in Bodoni type
on Simpson's eggshell text

LIBRARY OF CONGRESS CATALOG NUMBER 67-64346

Foreword

This publication undoubtedly will become a landmark since it constitutes the first systematic effort to determine, categorize, and describe those problem areas which superintendents of public schools perceive to be especially bothersome. Prior to this study, little attention had been given or systematic effort extended toward attempting to classify or understand the complex problems which the public school superintendent faces. This monograph discusses the present roles that the U. S. Office of Education, state departments of education, colleges and universities, regional educational laboratories, and selected professional associations perform in determining the most pressing problems faced by superintendents. In addition, the monograph indicates the nature of services and in-service training which are available for superintendents.

In the latter chapters of this monograph, the collected data are analyzed and interpreted in terms of the historical, political, and sociological causes of the present problems which face educational administrators. The final chapter concisely presents recommendations and suggestions for a course of action to help the superintendents.

This study is of especial interest to the U. S. Office of Education because of its content, findings, recommendations, and because of the fact that the study was proposed by the Office of Education. The University of Oregon was then encouraged to undertake such an endeavor. In its entirety, Dr. Keith Goldhammer, Associate Dean of the School of Education, designed and directed the project to its successful completion as attested by this publication.

HOWARD F. HJELM
Acting Director
Division of Elementary-
Secondary Research
Bureau of Research, USOE

GLENN C. BOERRIGTER
Research Coordinator, Research Branch
Division of Elementary-
Secondary Research
Bureau of Research, USOE

Acknowledgments

The research reported in this monograph was financed by a grant from the U. S. Office of Education (Project No. 6-2423, Grant No. OEG-4-6-062423-1720). The results of the study were first published as a final report to USOE.

There are many people and groups to whom the authors are deeply indebted for their cooperation. Particularly we are indebted to all of the superintendents, state superintendents, staff members of state departments of education, personnel from USOE, colleges and universities, AASA, and regional educational laboratories who participated in the study and gave of their time generously. Without their assistance and cooperation, this study would not have been possible.

Dr. Howard F. Hjelm, Acting Director of the Division of Elementary-Secondary Research, and Dr. Glenn C. Boerrigter, Research Coordinator of the same branch, were instrumental in the initiation of the study and were of untold assistance at all stages. They were particularly helpful, along with Dr. Ray Dethy, now of Northeastern University, in establishing schedules to expedite our work in Washington, D. C.

Dr. Jack Culbertson and Dr. Terry Eidell of UCEA rendered invaluable assistance in the formulation of the study, the review of conceptual materials related to the study, and the encouragement and suggestions which they made at various times during the study.

Special appreciation is expressed to Miss Margaret Nielsen, editor of the Bureau of Educational Research, University of Oregon, for her editorial assistance, her participation as a member of the team during the data analysis and writing stages and her checking on a host of details to assure the accuracy of the report.

Appreciation is also specially due Mrs. Joanne Kitchel, editor of the Center for the Advanced Study of Educational Administration, who edited the final draft and supervised the production of the monograph.

Dean Paul B. Jacobson assisted with interviews in the Chicago area, critically read the first draft of the report, and aided, as well, through his facilitation of the many arrangements necessary for the team to develop its materials.

The Center for the Advanced Study of Educational Administration, a research and development center sponsored by the United States Office of Education and the University of Oregon, made its resources available to us through all stages of the study and assumed major responsibility for the production of the monograph. Appreciation is expressed to the Executive Committee and the members of the staff for their assistance.

Finally, to Miss Sandra Harris, Project Secretary, we express a deep debt of gratitude. She served the needs of this project far beyond the call of duty while managing the affairs of the office, administering the details of all travel and field relationships, typing our copious notes, and even more ministering to our needs with a cheerful countenance and a willingness to assume the difficult burdens.

KEITH GOLDHAMMER
JOHN E. SUTTLE
WILLIAM D. ALDRIDGE
GERALD L. BECKER

August, 1967

UNIVERSITY OF OREGON, Eugene, Oregon

Contents

Some Abbreviations Used

AASA — American Association of School Administrators
ADA — Average Daily Attendance
ADC — Aid to Dependent Children
AFT — American Federation of Teachers
DCT — Department of Classroom Teachers
ESEA — Elementary and Secondary Education Act
NCATE — National Council for Accreditation of Teacher Education
NDEA — National Defense Education Act
NEA — National Education Association
OEO — Office of Economic Opportunity
PTA — Parent-Teachers Association
UCEA — University Council for Educational Administration
USOE — United States Office of Education

1 /

The Nature and
Purposes of the Study

The Dilemmas of Educational Administration

With the increasing ferment in education, attention has been focused upon the roles and the functions of the educational administrator, both in the operation of the schools and in the provision of that leadership which is essential for maintaining the viability of public education in a dynamically changing society. Since 1950, the training of educational administrators has drastically altered, indicating a major shift in emphasis among those who help to set the patterns of administration in this country. Whereas the training of administrators previously emphasized the technological problems of school management, the "new movement" has stressed the importance of administrative theory, the applications of the behavioral sciences to the problems of educational administration, the social context in which educational administration takes place, the analysis of the school organization as a social system, the analysis of the reciprocal relationships of diverse roles within the organization, and the interpretation of educational administration within the broader sphere of public administration of the public schools. Whereas before World War II the student who wished to prepare himself as an administrator selected courses in school buildings, school finance, school personnel administration, and other specialized studies deemed essential for technical operations, the student of today takes courses in administrative problems, the nature of administrative behavior, the politics of education, the schools as a social organization, and research and theory in educational administration.

Regardless of the emphasis upon the development of theory and the study of administration, the mundane problems of the public schools persist. The administrator in the public schools is faced daily with the task of assisting the school board, the subordinate administrators, the teachers, and the community in the solution of complex problems that arise out of both the operations of the public schools and the needs and dislocations of the broader society. The theory of administration might help the administrator to define his problems better and understand the structure of the social systems with which he must deal, but it does not necessarily help him to find the most appropriate strategies for maintaining the school as an agency fully responsive to and responsible for the educational needs of contemporary American life.

As never before, the administrator is forced to take cognizance of the problems that accumulate within his community as a result of both legislated and *de facto* segregation; of poverty and cultural deprivation; of the diverse aspirations and expectations of different segments of the community; of the varying educational needs of the community; of changing manpower needs and allocations; of the vast explosion of knowledge and the restructuring of many of the academic disciplines; of our national imperatives and international responsibilities; of the foment in the study of education and the encouragement of experimentation and innovation within the schools; of the unrest among minority groups, students, parents and teachers who no longer submit to being passive onlookers of the decision-making processes which affect them; and of the changing characteristics of the teaching profession and its ability to deal more effectively with the complex educational problems of children.

There are those who maintain that the superintendency as we now know it is a dysfunctional role in contemporary school organization. Some maintain that the chief executive of a large public school district must not be so much an educator as a business manager and public relations expert. In spite of the experience of the early part of this century when educational administration was divided between those responsible for the educational leadership and those in charge of the business management, there is a significant clamor today to divide the business and the educational management of the schools and to divorce the leadership functions of the chief executive from the educational management.

There are those who maintain that the contemporary administrator is a manager, and the schools would be better served if administration were divorced from program leadership, evaluation, and development. Like the hospital administrator, who performs managerial responsibilities, the educational administrator should really be a manager, a public relations agent, a person who is able to acquire increasing resources to meet the needs of the organization, and who manages the program for the allocation of those resources.

There are others who recognize that the school organization is now caught in the center of controversy among the various groups who have diverse values and educational aspirations. These individuals hold that the chief function of the educational administrator is political, acting as a mediator and attempting to achieve a high degree of stabilization of the school organization amidst the changing and conflicting patterns of community life.

There are still others who maintain that the educational enterprise is unique among the governmental functions of society, and the role of the educational administrator continues to be one which relates all aspects of management and operations to instructional effectiveness. The educational administrator, they hold, is primarily the administrator of an educational program, and he can be proficient in managing all other phases of the school program only to the extent that his central focus and competency are in the field of education.

The conflicts of perspectives exist not only within the profession, but within the broader society as well. The *Washington Post*, in a news story about the 1966 convention of the American Association of School Administrators, identified the crux of the problem when it described the convention as "a group of administrators in search of a purpose." The news media, when describing the bitter conflicts in which administrators are involved, now refer to "the old types" and "the new breed" of superintendents. The two genres are not well defined, and the same difficulties, conflicts, problems, and tragedies are experienced by both classifications, seemingly without discrimination.

If the study of administration has resulted in any hard knowledge, it is the importance of the administrator to the maintenance of the organization, the pointing of directions for the organization, and the establishment of a climate that is either conducive to or frustrating of change and adaptation. As various studies have pointed out, the administrator is in a position either to promote broad participation in decision-making and creativity on the part of individuals in the organization or to run a tight ship and discourage the efforts of any of the participants to rock the boat. The administrator does more than set the climate for the participants of the organization. He establishes certain goals; he allocates resources; he develops the criteria for the selection of personnel; he is the bridge between the organization and the broader society from which it derives the resources with which it has to operate. He controls the use of sanctions, both positive and negative, within the organization, and by his use of them, he establishes the determinants for the behavior of subordinates. To the extent that the organization is adaptive, it is likely that there will be an administrator at its helm who provokes and encourages creativity and innovation within it. To the extent that the organization drifts aimlessly, it is likely to have an administrative head who is indifferent or vacillating in his leadership role. To the extent that it is rigid and unadaptive, it is likely that there will be an administrator at its helm who restricts activity within relatively inflexible bounds. These types of school districts exist in varying degrees in every state of the country. But the need persists for measures which will improve the quality of education rapidly in every part of the country. Whether or not the necessary changes occur depends to a considerable extent upon, first, whether or not the leadership of educational administrators becomes sufficiently effective to cope with the problems and, second, whether or not the dislocations that now appear to exist between the needs of contemporary educational organization, and historically-rooted definitions of administrative functions in education are resolved.

The Purposes of This Study

This study developed from an assumption that superintendents of schools have not as yet made the adjustments in their roles indicated by the changing demands made upon them by society and by the teaching profession. One reason for the lack of progress toward their role adaptation is that those who might best assist them have not focused their attention upon the problems which superintendents perceive to be most critical. As a result the superintendent has long been the object of considerable criticism but not the recipient of much meaningful assistance by those who have the resources to help him.

This study, then, is an attempt to describe contemporary and emergent problems of educational administration as confronted and percevied by the superintendents of schools, to discuss the manner in which preparatory and in-service training programs prepare educational administrators to deal with these problems and to suggest means through which both governmental and non-governmental education agencies, such as state departments of education, the United States Office of Education, professional educational organizations, and colleges and universities may help bridge the gaps.

Specifically, the purposes of this study may be stated as follows:

(1) To analyze and categorize those problems which school superintendents perceive as basic to the effective operation of their schools;

(2) To analyze the various programs which have been developed by institutions of higher education, state departments of education, and other educational agencies for the preparatory and in-service training of school administrators and the relationship of these programs to the needs of school superintendents today;

(3) On the basis of these findings to suggest how the roles and responsibilities of educational agencies, such as the United States Office of Education, state departments of education, colleges and universities and professional organizations, may be adapted to (a) maintain a continuous identification of the major problems and issues confronting the administration of the public schools, (b) establish priorities for the support and stimulation of research related to these problems, (c) develop structures and processes for the application of knowledge to the solutions of major problems and the formulation of appropriate administrative technologies and strategies, and (d) establish working relationships among all such agencies and local school districts.

Design of the Study

The procedures for the study were as follows:

(1) A thorough review was made of the current literature of educational administration related to the level of the superintendency. A perusal of this literature revealed studies in which typical problems of school administrators were identified. This information was used to make preliminary identification of issues which might arise and to formulate approaches both to the direction of the conferences and the preparation for the individual interviews.[1]

(2) The director of the study spent three weeks in Washington, D.C., to study the programs, policies, and operating procedures of USOE, particularly as they relate to the problems of educational administrators.

---

[1] A supplement to the final report to USOE will report the findings of this phase of the study.

He also interviewed officials of AASA and staff members of a Congressional subcommittee which was currently studying USOE.

(3) Five one-day conferences of school superintendents were held in different geographical areas. The main purposes of the conferences were to open discussions of the problems of administrators as they perceive them, to attain rapport between the administrators and the research staff, and to establish a foundation upon which depth interviews with all of the superintendents could be based. The conferences were held in San Francisco, Oklahoma City, Chicago, New York, and Atlanta. The five locations were selected in cooperation with USOE so as to secure data from various sections of the country and from a sample of the several states located in each section. Because of limitations of time and resources, it was decided to select eight to ten superintendents to participate in each conference. In all, 47 superintendents, representing 22 states, participated in the study. Also present at each of the conferences were representatives from two or three state departments of education in the area. Thirteen state departments of education were involved. A few observers also attended the conferences. These included representatives from USOE, the University Council for Educational Administration, and various colleges and universities. A transcript was made of each conference by a certified court reporter.

Since a limited number of superintendents was to be interviewed, careful selection was imperative. The following criteria were used to screen nominees:

(a) Superintendents must be representatives of various states and various sized school districts. Four categories of districts were selected for representation: those with average daily attendance of 3,000 to 10,000; those with ADA of 10,000 to 25,000; those with ADA of 25,000 to 50,000; and those with ADA of more than 50,000.

(b) Superintendents selected should reflect the points of view typical of the size of district which they represent.

(c) Superintendents should be limited to those who actively participate in professional activities outside of their own school districts and are recognized for their leadership within their states or in the nation.

(d) School superintendents selected should be able to verbalize their points of view effectively.

(e) Superintendents should have had at least five years in the superintendency.

(f) Superintendents should be located within a radius of approximately 150 miles of the conference site. (This criterion was flexibly administered.)

Lists of superintendents were obtained from colleges and universities, state departments of education, and educational leaders. Every person or agency requested to submit lists did so, and each list identified both names and special qualifications of the superintendents suggested as candidates.

Following the receipt of the lists, names were selected to assure representation from the various states and sizes of school districts. Nominees were also screened on the basis of their reported qualifications and nomination from more than one source.

(4) Following each conference, each participant was interviewed in depth, in order to permit him to expand upon the topics which he presented at the conference and to introduce new material which he had not then had an opportunity to introduce. Interview guides were prepared, but not rigidly followed (See Appendix B). The interviews were intended to be open-ended and only partially directive. Prior to the conference each participant was sent a discussion guide in which he could list the problems he wanted to bring to the attention of the group, with space provided for taking notes at the conference and for preparing materials for the interview.

Interviewers made careful notes of the discussion and dictated them for transcription as soon after the interview as possible. In three instances, superintendents were unavoidably prevented from attending the conference after they had accepted the invitation, but all were later contacted and interviewed.

(5) During the time of the research team's work in each of the conference areas, representatives of various colleges and universities were also interviewed relative to their administrative preparation, research, and in-service education programs. Colleges and universities were selected in cooperation with USOE and UCEA. These institutions were chosen on the basis of their having recognized administrative preparation programs, their assuming major responsibility for the preparation of administrators in their states or localities, and their proximity to the conference site. In all, 36 colleges and universities from 21 states were represented.

(6) The research team also interviewed representatives of regional educational laboratories located in each conference area. Interviews were

made in six regional laboratories. Plans had been made for interviews in a seventh laboratory, but respondents failed to keep the appointments.

The data collected through the transcripts of the conferences and the interview schedules were subjected to careful content analysis. Each member of the research team assumed responsibility for the content analysis and organization of the data in a specific portion of the report.

2/

Superintendents' Perceptions of Their Problems

Introduction

The central focus of this phase of the study was on administrative problems as perceived by the superintendents. These men were asked to give a forthright analysis of the problems they were currently experiencing in their own school districts and to avoid attempting to identify the great problems and issues which confront the field of education generally throughout the country. The emphasis was upon their identification of problems from the vantage point of the roles which they perform in the school organization.

The problems which superintendents identified are not necessarily the most critical problems confronting education in the United States today. The fact remains, however, that since they did identify these problems, they constitute issues with which the superintendent must deal, and they represent areas of operations to which superintendents are willing to assign high priorities and allocate increased resources in order to find solutions. Much of the time and effort of those who are concerned with governance of school districts is occupied with these problems.

The review of the data indicated that there were several different schemes which could be used for the categorization of the problems. The scheme finally adopted appears best to represent the ways in which the superintendents themselves regarded the interrelationships among problems.

The problems can be grouped in six categories:

(1) EDUCATIONAL CHANGE. A great deal of the thought of the superintendents focused upon the many influences pressing upon them and the public schools to stimulate change in the schools. Superintendents feel that many of their problems arise from shifting expectations for the schools within the community as well as from the interventions of agencies outside of the schools. They are equally concerned with the fact that there are pressures for change from within the organization itself.

(2) TEACHER MILITANCY. One of the most severe problems besetting administrators is the growing militancy of teachers and their professional organizations. In an earlier age, Willard Waller could hold that the community image of the teacher was as the modern counterpart of the Roman Vestal Virgins, but in the minds of the superintendents this would certainly not be true today. The problems of dealing with militant teacher groups who demand a role in the decision-making structure of the schools have impressed a whole new set of concerns upon the superintendent. These problems change the nature of the school organization and create new definitions of the limitations and potentialities of public school programs.

(3) INSTRUCTION. Among all their other concerns, superintendents emphasized that schools exist to teach the young. How the school will continue to teach the young and toward what ends are matters of considerable concern. It is apparent that the conflicts and controversies that beset the superintendent are not entirely on the governmental or organizational levels. He is deeply involved in and concerned with problems of curriculum, instructional services of all sorts, evaluation, adaptation and learning outcomes.

(4) ADMINISTRATIVE LEADERSHIP. All of these problems imply for most administrators that the times require changes in the nature of the leadership functions of the superintendency and new demands on his competency. He seems to be forced to consider not only these issues and their impacts upon the schools, but also the major role he is required to play within the community and the school organization because of these issues.

(5) CRITICAL SOCIAL ISSUES. Since the Supreme Court Decision of 1954, it has been apparent to many educators that schools can no longer retreat into their ivy-covered cloisters for protection from the contro-

versies of contemporary social issues. If there was any doubt about this ten years ago, it has now been thoroughly dissipated. But there are still problems related to the ways in which the schools operate in the market-place of social conflict and the appropriateness of their being so in-volved. The issues of church and state, of desegregation, of the more equitable distribution of economic resources, of the reduction of social distance among cultural and racial groups—all involve the schools and create new demands not only upon the programs of the schools but also upon the nature of the decisions which have to be made in the mainte-nance and operation of the schools. As the "face" of the school organi-zation to the community, the superintendent today frequently feels that he is more involved in social than in purely educational issues.

(6) FINANCE. The traditional role of the administrator as the procurer of resources for the school organization has not been greatly changed. As we shall presently see, financial worries still plague the superintendent and are a primary problem for him.

This chapter will consider in some detail superintendents' perceptions of each of these central areas of concern. Insofar as possible, the state-ments of the problems will be made in the manner in which the super-intendents expressed them.

Educational Change

Societal and community changes

American society is experiencing rapid change, and the schools are caught in the flow. One superintendent stated that "there seems to be a general unrest of mankind throughout the world." Nations are look-ing for recognition, and people are seeking their rights. Within the United States, mobility has become a way of life for a large percentage of the population. Modern technology presents the schools with an ex-citing array of new instructional devices which might well change the entire structure of education, but about which school personnel are ig-norant. Schools are being asked to do things that they have never before been asked to do, while they continue to perform their traditional roles.

Urbanization is a facet of the complex process of current societal change. Rural areas, dominated by agriculture, are becoming increasingly industrialized, resulting in rapid and frequently traumatic upsets in traditional social, political, economic and cultural patterns. Problems of one sort develop in the metropolitan area itself, while different sorts of problems arise in the "bedroom neighborhoods" surrounding the city. The central city may contain the industry, but the managers live out of the district in the suburbs. "The leadership of our district lives outside of the community." Superintendents are concerned about the impact that non-resident power and influence may have upon the schools, and particularly upon the quality of school board membership. Whereas in the past the people who had an economic stake in the community were a primary reference group for superintendents, these people may no longer be greatly concerned about the public schools. In this shifting situation, the superintendent finds himself unsure of what to expect, to whom to go for advice and how to act.

As people move around, they are exposed to many kinds of educational programs. Partly as a result of this exposure, people expect more from their schools. Blind faith in the schools is gone; more people question what is going on. This questioning of the schools has virtually forced school personnel to take a hard look at educational programs. There is a resulting self-criticism in education and an endeavor to evaluate ongoing programs to see if they are actually accomplishing what they are supposed to accomplish. The situation is such that professional educators "cannot decide by themselves what the schools' role is to be." There must be broad involvement in this decision, but at present the catalysts which could bring groups together to resolve the issues are lacking. In most communities it is the superintendent who must gather information for various interested groups in the community and "provide leadership as to what he feels is the best educational program for the kids."

In spite of the pressure placed upon the schools by societal changes, the schools are slow to change. According to one superintendent, this is due to the fact that one of the traditional functions of the school has been the preservation of the cultural heritage. "The school itself is struggling to discover what in its system it must maintain and what is necessary to throw out." Complicating these decisions is the task of deciding between the needs of society as opposed to the needs of individuals. Although the superintendent may feel that changes must be made on the basis of the needs of individual children, he also feels considerable pressure from a "push toward national goals." These, he feels, are conflicts which must be resolved.

Federal influences affecting educational change

Under provisions of the federal Civil Rights Act of 1965 and the Elementary and Secondary Education Act of 1965, the role of the federal government in education has greatly expanded. The new roles of the federal government in relation to local school districts are met by the superintendents with mixed emotions. The feelings of the superintendents were well expressed in the words of one of them, who said, in explaining the reaction of his community:

> There has been a general reaction in the community to federal programs, some positive and some negative. A good part of the community is against the Great Society and the amount of money being spent. On the other hand, many feel that here is money to be taken and educational support is needed, and there is no denying that some things have come about that would not have come about without federal aid.

Most superintendents do not feel that local participation in federal programs is actually voluntary. They see federal programs as "local money coming back and if we don't spend it, it's lost." One superintendent stated that the United States Office of Education asked Congress for "a great deal of money in order to make sure that they got some." They received more than they had planned for, and along with the large sums of money went "control and power."

The major fear expressed by the superintendents centers, as might be expected, around the issue of increasing federal control of education with a corresponding loss of local control. Superintendents reported that their school boards had deep suspicions about what the federal government was trying to accomplish. Some superintendents recognized that school boards have a "semi-proprietary" attitude toward the schools and fear the federal intrusion into their domain. "Actually, control is present when money is designated for certain types of programs. It gets districts to do certain things in specific areas." "We'll get so dependent on this money that we'll have to take it and do what the federal government says." The threatened withholding of funds by the USOE under the Civil Rights Act to insure that certain conditions be met has reinforced these fears.

Administrators do not want the federal government involved in prescribing curriculum, determining building specifications, determining criteria for the employment of personnel, or in any other way interfering with decisions that traditionally have been made on the local level. They feel that if federal funds are earmarked for support of particular programs, the local district should be allowed to draw up its own guidelines for the program.

Categorical aid came under particularly heavy attack. It is a general feeling that the federal government should provide general aid based upon some index of need rather than specifying in what areas the money must be spent. Superintendents point out that federal funds generally cannot be used to support and improve district programs already begun, and that this is a definite weakness in federal aid programs. Schools are faced with inadequacies in their current programs while rushing into new federally financed programs which they may not be able to continue if federal support is withdrawn.

Although superintendents generally feel that perhaps their leadership ability in program development is abrogated by categorical aid, a few readily admitted that without categorical aid the funds would probably have been used to offset budgetary problems with the result that progress would have been less than what has occurred. Several admitted that they favored categorical aid because it removed the necessity for argument with the school board for the allocation of funds to new programs and enabled them to initiate programs for which the board or community had previously refused to provide funds.

A variety of problems has arisen concerning the federal programs, many of them centering around technical questions. Initially, the administrators had to spend a disproportionate amount of time in preparing proposals. Elaborate application procedures, endless delays, and inappropriate timing of funding, and deadlines for report-making were frustrating. Some districts received evaluation questionnaires before they had received funds to begin the operation of programs. There is a general feeling among superintendents that USOE is in need of much more coordination of its various departments in handling federal funds.

One of the central problems for superintendents has arisen from the lack of coordination between the requirements of federal programs and the operational patterns of the schools. Administrators have had to "skim off" regular personnel to be used in these programs, which frequently have been initiated in the middle of the school year. According to the superintendents, the new programs under ESEA rarely give them the lead time which they need in order to plan adequately for the programs .

Staffing problems which have resulted from federal programs were so severe in some instances that superintendents raised doubts about the advisability of continuation of the programs. Superintendents were particularly disturbed because in many instances they lost personnel to state departments of education and other school districts which had different types of federal programs. Salaries of people so recruited were much higher than could be afforded with district funds. School districts which do not have federal programs are particularly adversely affected.

The inconsistency of federal attitudes in implementing programs was also noted. It was reported that some districts received praise from one team of federal coordinators for a given program, yet when they re-applied for that same program, they received very negative comments from the agency processing the application. There were complaints that, first, school people were not allowed to record the race of a student; then, they were told to keep records on each race separately. Inconsistency was also evidenced in application procedures. For some projects only a one-page application was required; for other projects, application procedures were very complex and the cost of their preparation to school districts was high.

Another feeling of superintendents which relates to the issue of consistency is their sense of remoteness from USOE. Superintendents like to operate in a situation of mutual interaction with persons who make decisions affecting their proposals, but the USOE is an "outside agency" with whom the superintendent "cannot deal." "It's impossible to arrive at a compromise with this foreign agency as I do in other issues that involve only local or closer agencies."

Other specific problems mentioned by superintendents were:

(1) *What do you do with staffs of terminated federal programs when the staff members are on tenure?*

(2) *Why doesn't the government include funds for preventative programs as well as for remedial ones?*

(3) *How does the superintendent comply with certain conditions in project guidelines which are contrary to state laws?*

(4) *How does the superintendent obtain needed Title I money when it is allocated on the basis of the number of people in a district receiving aid to dependent children?* The district with a large number of state employees, who are not allowed to collect such aid, is discriminated against.

In general, superintendents favor the goals of federally financed programs. They want to feel closer to USOE, however, and they definitely want greater coordination of federal programs. They feel that if they were better able to express their needs, problems, and concerns to USOE personnel with whom they had consistent, face-to-face rapport, they could use federal funds more effectively.

State and local pressures

Through legislative enactments, the regulations of state boards, and the policies of the state departments of education, the state exerts pressures on the schools. The legislatures, at the request of special interest groups, "meddle in the curriculum" by passing acts relating to such topics as the teaching of Communism and "the free enterprise system." This problem is apparently not universal among the states, but to the superintendents involved it is a serious violation of authority which they feel should properly belong to professional educators.

The establishment of accreditation standards by state departments of education is used as a means of moving schools in directions which state departments deem desirable. New standards are frequently "much higher than they were before," but additional moneys fail to accompany the imposition of higher standards. This creates a crisis for some school districts. For instance, in one state new accreditation standards specified that every child must have physical education, where previously this had been optional in the upper levels of high school. To meet these standards, the district will have to divert money from the elementary school budget. This problem can be eliminated if budgetary allocations are required to accompany an accreditation bill as it goes to the legislature.

Unceasing growth is a community change with which the schools must deal. In one community the schools are faced with an increase in student enrollment of "2500 and more per year." In this district of about 18,000 pupils there are always more students than the faculty can house; consequently, it has become "standard procedure" to bond to capacity and then "throw in with the state to handle needs beyond that." Growth problems in this community will continue to increase in the near future, since a new rapid transit system will have a terminal there.

Yet, even this rate of growth appears insignificant when compared to the growth of a metropolitan area such as Chicago. It was estimated that during the decade of Dr. Benjamin Willis' tenure as superintendent, the city school system grew by about 200 to 300 thousand students. A respondent pointed out that this increase is greater than the total enrollment of over 95 per cent of the city school districts in the United States.

The general national trend toward consolidation and annexation gives added impetus to the problems of district growth, and "as the district grows arithmetically, the problems increase geometrically." The superintendent is faced with the problem of bringing new groups of parents together; new staff people are interacting, and new relationships must be established. A tremendous increase in human relations problems occurs and these problems have to be dealt with. With the increased size of his district, the superintendent feels that he just does not have the time to study the problems and work out solutions to them.

Building may or may not become a problem in a school district. It is interesting to note that one superintendent of a large Eastern city in which the population has doubled in the past 15 years, does not feel that building is a problem. The board has "continually planned ahead and kept up with building needs." Even though at least four or five buildings per year have been required, the people have consistently voted in favor of bond elections.

On the other hand, the superintendent of a large Southwestern city which has experienced rapid growth says that buildings constitute a serious problem for his district. Some of his schools are surplus military barracks, and at the present time the district has "6 million dollars to do 12 million dollars worth of needed building." The people whose children attend school in these old barracks, dating back to World War II, are dissatisfied; community pressure for children to attend new, attractive buildings runs high; yet, the district has only half the needed building funds.

The factors which might account for the differences in attitude demonstrated by the above two communities were not mentioned by the superintendents. It is likely that such discrepancies arise both from legal obstacles to the procurement of adequate capital funds and community concerns about increased taxation and inequities resulting from obsolescent tax structures.

The changing nature of intergovernmental relationships is another problem which manifests itself in the community. The school is being "forced into cooperative relationships with other community agencies without having any real basis for maintaining satisfactory relationships." For some superintendents this goes against both "feelings and training." There is apparently very little coordination among city, county, and school operations, with a considerable amount of friction and duplication of functions among agencies as a consequence. In areas where city officials are inefficient or ineffective, the school may be considered "guilty of mismanagement by association."

The administration of the schools in large, complex urban communities is no longer independent of the government of the municipality even if it is fiscally independent. The most critical problems which confront the urban schools are pressing community issues in which various municipal agencies are also involved. They make decisions which have major impacts upon the schools. As one superintendent said, "Our big urban centers today are governed by wheels within wheels. Nothing is streamlined." The result is that superintendents and school boards frequently are advised of decisions after they are made and have to adapt the educational program and their planning accordingly. When issues are not resolved, the school board and superintendent are sometimes made "the fall guys" for the politicians. This is particularly true in regard to highly volatile issues, such as desegregation, war on poverty programs, and urban renewal projects.

Some schools are pressed by the community to move into programs before school personnel are really ready to accept them. The board and the community hear "so much propaganda" about certain programs that they cannot understand why the school is not moving into them. Community Action Groups and Economic Opportunity Boards exert pressure on the school board and are at times publically critical of board and superintendent actions.

In summary, the school is being forced into different relationships with community and governmental groups; finding ways to handle effectively these new relationships is a problem which the superintendent must face.

Organizing for change

Organizing to meet and direct change is one of the responsibilities which troubles superintendents. That this is an area of deep concern was demonstrated by a superintendent who asked, "How do you implement? How do you get going? How do you get the district ready for innovation?"

The superintendent himself may be a powerful barrier to change in the district. There are those "who are willing to take a chance in convincing their board that change is necessary." There are also those "who operate on the basis that they must maintain the *status quo*." It was suggested that there needs to be greater cooperation and coordination among superintendents. By such cooperative action similar approaches and programs can be developed in neighboring areas, and the stronger superintendents can give support and assistance to their colleagues who fear advancing into new programs. It was proposed that universities should take the lead in organizing retraining programs for superintendents. Retraining "needs to become as common in educational administration as it now is in business."

Superintendents express concern that they find personnel to be extremely resistant to change, yet the social sciences tell them that man is the most adaptable of all animals. Once a program is disseminated throughout the district, it is difficult to "shore up these changes and maintain them." However, some superintendents have found that "the key to innovation is total involvement." The staff is "more competent than previously realized," and when they are involved in planning for a change from its earliest stages they become committed to the program which results in greater changes. "The more the total staff is involved in innovation, the less dictatorial the decisions that are necessary and the less the resistance to the change."

There is general agreement that it is necessary for superintendents to plan for change and that staff time be allocated for planning. There is a "tremendous need for getting schools involved in research," and this can do much to establish an atmosphere in which innovation is stimulated. Change cannot be facilitated through traditional schedules for the staff and traditional budgetary allocations in school districts. If innovation and change are going to be successful, the staff will have to be freed from other responsibilities and given the time they need to plan, prepare materials, and inaugurate new programs and techniques. This type of organization will cost more money, but it will enable staff to work effectively on professional problems. Better communication among all levels of the organization will have to be established. The superintendents indicated that if administrators and teaching staff are so rigidly scheduled that they are unable to plan beyond the week to week program, there will not be much innovation in that system and new programs will have little chance for survival.

Teacher Militancy

Power of teacher organizations

Teachers as a group are now demanding a greater voice in policy formulation, especially on matters which relate to instruction and teacher welfare. Although this movement appears to be general across the nation, some distinctions were noted in the intensity of concern among superintendents in various parts of the country. The most intense reactions were apparent in the areas represented at the Chicago and New York conferences, where there has been the longest history of teacher militancy. The sentiment seemed to be of least magnitude in the areas represented at the Atlanta conference. Here it was felt that the primary problem facing teacher associations was the elimination of dual, segregated organizations which consumed much of their energy. In the South-east it was also felt that if the superintendents found means for making desirable organizational adaptations to incorporate teachers in the decision-making process, some of the ill effects of teacher militancy in other parts of the country could be avoided. One Southern superintendent said, "We should look upon this as a challenge and an opportunity, not as an evil."

The feelings of some superintendents seem to run very high concerning the topic of teacher associations because of the impetus they have given to collective negotiations and teacher militancy. They state that teachers' organizations were built and encouraged by superintendents for professional reasons. These reasons included the development of teaching as a profession, the encouragement of professional planning and development through group action, the stimulation of research and development in education, the support of progressive educational legislation, and the increase in resources available to education. Most of the administrators in the sample acknowledged that the status of the teaching profession until after World War II was deplorable and that superintendents felt that the condition of education and the status of the teaching profession could be up-graded through the improvement of the professional image and competence of teachers.

Now, superintendents say that the teachers have taken over the professional associations. They are driving the superintendents out and making their associations "activist" organizations exclusively concerned with the economic benefits and other welfare provisions for teachers. One superintendent compared the situation in education today to the Boston Tea Party. "Teachers are now encouraged to find things wrong in the school program. It's a part of the game they are now expected to play." "Effort is being made by the leaders of the professional educational associations to create friction between the teachers and the administrative staff." Superintendents viewed the educational profession as formerly unified, with teachers and administrators engaged cooperatively in the same pursuits, but occupying different but coordinated roles. Although they rationalize the present chasm by ascribing it to the efforts of a loud minority," they, nevertheless, fear that education will suffer as a result of the gulf that is being created between the teachers and the administrators.

The growing bent toward "unionism" regardless of the affiliation of the teachers' organization draws a sharp distinction between the administrator and the teacher. One superintendent said that merit salary increases were discouraged by superintendents because of their fear of upsetting the "team idea" in education. However, he fears that "unionism is going to do the same thing."

Many superintendents claim that the problem of the teachers' movement arises out of the "competition between the NEA and the AF of T." The present push has "been sparked by union organizations in competition with teacher organizations." "The NEA is running scared of the union and looking for means by which it can outdo the unions." Competition becomes particularly acute when the superintendent must deal with more than one teacher association in his district.

Teacher preparation for participation in professional organizations

Teacher preparation programs are also accorded a measure of blame for the militancy problem. Teacher training institutions "should accept the main responsibility of providing the teacher with the big picture." In one district the teachers attempted to cut administrators' salaries as a means of increasing teacher salaries. This superintendent feels that if the teachers had been instructed to see "the overall picture" in the district and had some understanding of organizational and administrative procedures, they would have known that even eliminating the central office staff would benefit them very little financially. "There is a definite deficiency in the teacher training program when teachers are not able to see the complexity of the educational system."

It was suggested that the university, in dealing with this problem, should take action by "stressing the personal satisfaction of teaching." The goal of education is not to provide everything optimal for teachers, but for the children. It should be pointed out by the university that the primary purpose of teachers' organizations should be to improve the instructional process. The university must also develop selection procedures to insure that we get "more quality people in the profession." The implication here is that "quality people" will not be as militant, will be better able to "see the big picture," and will be more interested in improving instruction than in teacher welfare. Such teachers will cause fewer problems for the superintendent.

Negotiation laws

Legally required negotiation procedures produce an additional problem. The disruption or removal of existing, efficient means of reaching decisions with teachers results in resentment among superintendents. "The [negotiations] bill sets up legal camps, and we can't use our committees the way we used to." The negotiations bill "fouled all of our procedures up," and the teachers want to go back to the old way. In addition, some superintendents feel that it is a mistake to select a single bargaining agent and "close the door on other representatives."

A basic concern of superintendents in the negotiations process is deciding what issues are negotiable. Some of the negotiation laws which have been passed are so general that they have "made teachers feel there isn't anything that can't be negotiated." Different communities have negotiated different issues, and "everything that is negotiated in some other community becomes an item for negotiation in our community." This has resulted in negotiating documents of over 50 pages during the first year of negotiations, with hardly any item excluded from the process. "It [the professional association] wants the teachers now to feel that they can negotiate on everything, and this constitutes a major problem for the superintendent."

Most superintendents feel that they are at a disadvantage in the negotiation process. To a considerable extent, the larger and central school districts in each state have become battlefields for the national and state organizations which are competing for teacher memberships. After winning recognition, the organizations must continue to demonstrate to teachers that they can "bring home the bacon." They are staffed by experienced, professional negotiators and research specialists who assist local units. School boards and superintendents, on the other hand, are neophytes and amateurs in bargaining. The role of educational management in the negotiations process is not, as yet, well established. Many superintendents feel that the leadership of their national organization is a captive of the National Education Association and not in a position to give them the assistance the NEA provides for the teachers.

An important result of formalized negotiations procedures, frequently mentioned by the superintendents, is a shift in attitude on the part of the board. Whereas the board was formerly strongly in favor of improving teacher benefits, the board now fights the teachers for anything they get. Even in a district where negotiations are still in the offing, the board is not approving teachers' requests, even though it is not opposed to them, simply because it is "holding back a few trump cards so we can play the game."

The problem of time is one almost universally mentioned by the superintendents with regard to negotiation. One Eastern superintendent quoted one of his board members as saying in a speech that he had attended 80 negotiations sessions during the previous year and that his board was now embroiled again in negotiations. In another instance, five board members had two meetings a week from the first of January through the thirtieth of May. Six hundred hours per year in negotiations is not an unusual amount of time in the large metropolitan districts. This, of course, raises the question of whether or not board members and/or superintendents should be directly involved in the negotiations process. Superintendents fear that if the board is to be involved in such time-consuming process, qualified persons will not want to serve on school boards, and it is likely that the quality of school board membership will deteriorate. A particular concern of superintendents is that the new militancy of teachers is making school boards more politically minded than educationally oriented.

There was little agreement among the superintendents as to what course to follow regarding negotiations. Many felt that superintendents should provide channels of communication and opportunities for teachers to discuss problems and become involved whenever possible in the decision-making processes of the educational program. They felt that where negotiations is not a legal requirement, the superintendents would be wise to provide situations which would make negotiation unnecessary. Others stated that the "strong superintendent" would not "accede to the pressures," and that he would see that educational issues are solved "on the basis of educational principles."

The new demands imposed the burden upon the superintendent of devising some organizational structures and processes which have not been customary in education. As one superintendent summarized:

> We're going to have to spend some time on the development of adequate grievance procedures. The district that doesn't develop some adequate grievance procedures here is in for real trouble. We don't have any systematic procedures for helping the teacher to understand how he can stay within the organization when he has a real grievance. Where does the teacher go if he doesn't get satisfaction at the building level? Where does he go if he has a problem that he can't discuss with his principal or where the principal has made some error that is of a personal nature and the teacher feels that he cannot discuss it with him? If we do not have systematic procedures, the individual has no alternative but to go to the AF of T or the DCT. Because of organizational constraints he isn't sure that he should go over the principal's head to the assistant superintendent. It is very difficult to work out these grievance procedures in the professional organization and we're going to have to establish a structure that is realistic. I have been thinking of the possibility of something like the "ombudsman."

General attitude of superintendents
toward teacher militancy

Superintendents repeatedly indicated that they were unsure as to their position in the negotiations process. Some had decided for themselves what their role should be, but there was virtually no agreement among them. A large group of superintendents felt "caught in the middle." These men are apparently groping uncertainly for a satisfactory method of handling a situation for which their training and experience have not prepared them. They are looking hopefully to the time when the groups involved, the AASA, NEA, and AFT, will develop some ground rules on how to conduct negotiations properly.

Not all superintendents feel that the rising militancy of teacher organizations will be detrimental to education. Several men expressed the feeling that after this period of turmoil and uncertainty. education will be much stronger because of the increased teacher participation. Some superintendents see teacher militancy as a "resource." They state that the participation of teachers in the decision-making processes of the district is something which they have "been trying to accomplish for a long time."

Negotiations problems can be solved at the local level if we "follow through sincerely with our approach to the involvement of teachers in our decision-making.

> We have to have a commitment to the improvement of the profession and a genuine concern for the incorporation of teachers in the decision-making process. A part of our present problem is that we have a blind administrative approach and boards of education who cannot see the degree to which teachers can make the responsible decisions in which they are seeking to become involved.

These men seem to be saying that if administrators will actually practice the principles of sound human relations, the critical problems of militancy will disappear; the causes of teacher militancy will have been eliminated.

Instruction

Quality and supply of personnel

The shortage of qualified staff is a basic problem throughout the states, and superintendents find it necessary to recruit more extensively than ever before. The demand for more teachers is partly due to the population explosion and partly due to the expansion of knowledge. In addition, more time is required on the part of teachers for preparation of class materials, for coordination of course work with other department members and for supervision of instruction.

There is considerable competition for quality personnel among school districts, institutions of higher education (especially junior colleges), and industry. Industry is frequently able to skim off the top people because it offers higher salaries. Larger districts attract teachers from the smaller rural areas, leaving the small districts in a quandary. Many positions are filled with "bodies only." Good people are on the move either into administrative positions or into specialized positions which offer higher salaries. It was indicated that the elementary school preparatory programs drive the men out. The men who do go into elementary school teaching do so as a stepping stone to a principalship.

The pre-service training of teachers is considered by the superintendents to be a universal problem. There are broad differences in the quality of graduates from teachers colleges within and among the states. Many teachers are not prepared to do the job that is expected of them; they are not aware of the practical problems which they face, and many become lost or discouraged and leave the field. Superintendents feel that there is considerable surface teaching in education courses and insufficient involvement in varied classroom experiences. Only a limited amount of what is learned is applicable in practice.

Many superintendents feel that a different type of teacher may now be needed in the classroom. Youngsters, they say, are different today, and the traditional approach of teaching seems lacking in effectiveness. There are barriers present in the teaching-learning situation, such as language, economic and cultural differences, and diverse value-orientations toward education which may be ameliorated through the competence, skills, and supporting attitudes of the teachers.

Some of the superintendents charged that a lack of dedication to the teaching profession and to the ideology of educating all children exists among teachers. Many female teachers are not professionally oriented toward their jobs. Some are married, have children, and feel their first responsibility is to their home and youngsters rather than to the school. There also is a lack of interest and participation among teachers in professional activities and cultural programs. College training programs must be developed to build these values and attitudes, superintendents assert. Local districts also must carry some of the responsibility for practice-teacher and internship programs, in-service activities, screening, placement, and provision of guidance and counseling for teachers. Not all of the problems of quality were related to classroom teachers.

Many superintendents contend that it is difficult to find principals who are able to give the needed instructional leadership. Principals often lack qualities of flexibility, creativeness, and competence in making decisions, and many of them seem to avoid experimentation or deviation from traditional programs. It is charged that principals often do not initiate policies for fear of incurring criticism from dissident lay groups. Superintendents also blame colleges for not training leaders who are competent to deal with all the problems now facing the schools, and it is particularly disconcerting to large city superintendents that they they cannot find principals who are specifically trained to deal with the problems of education in the inner core of metropolitan centers.

Superintendents recognize that the school district also has a responsibility to its teachers for financial support. Superintendents find it difficult to make the public aware of the relationship that exists between salary level and the quality of teachers. A raise of a few hundred dollars on a salary schedule is not enough to make significant changes in securing well qualified personnel. A drastic overhaul of the total salary program is necessary to do the job, and it must be accomplished soon.

Finally, the lack of reciprocity in teacher certification among states seems to be an irritant for a number of superintendents. Since there are no uniform teaching certification requirements acceptable to all states and colleges, certificated teachers who move from one state to another may find it necessary to obtain temporary certification until they are able to complete courses which are required by the state to which they have moved. Many of these courses are not designed to improve a teacher's classroom competence, but are so much "filler" in a listing of course requirements. Those teachers who would rather take other courses to improve their skills still must choose these "filler" courses because certification is imperative. State certification requirements must take into account the increasing mobility of teachers and their need for improved professional competence.

Curriculum

A major concern of a number of superintendents was the development of a curriculum in accordance with the needs of the youth of the community which maintains balance and consistency between grade levels and subject areas. The youth within a community are in a state of flux and "we're not going to be teaching the same kind of kids tomorrow as we are teaching today." The percentage of college-bound youth is growing in most communities, and curriculum development seems to be following this trend by becoming increasingly academically oriented. Considerable support is given to this movement by secondary teachers and parents whose attitudes are strongly focused on academics. However, several superintendents indicated that they needed to provide more vocational and technical training in the schools as their communities become more highly industrialized. But superintendents are finding that vocational programs are expensive, lacking in prestige and "a very difficult product to sell."

Change also implies direction, and most superintendents hesitate to point out that "right way." As one superintendent put it:

> We are charged with the responsibility of justifying to the board of education which direction the district should go with its programs. We feel very insecure in taking a stand as to direction. Research does not indicate direction, and what research there is has not been well done and is insufficient in national coverage to give any assurance of a foundation upon which to base a decision. Therefore, the direction we take is based upon our feelings as to the way it should go, which is meager evidence to present to board.

A few superintendents pointed out the dangers of "bandwagonitis" which is leading school districts "down the road in pursuit" of a vast array of diverse programs, such as transformational grammar, linguistics, SMSG mathematics, BSCS biology, PSSC physics, and others. Some staff members become enthusiastically involved, others not at all, and some take a more conservative middle-of-the-road view. The results are confusion, much fragmentation of professional effort, and the hasty establishment of a number of tracks for a student to follow regardless of his preparation for them. One superintendent indicated that the schools should be a little behind the social order but somewhat at the edge of change. The facilities and instructional materials should not be exclusively modern he said, but should provide both old and modern so that students can see change.

The lack of emphasis upon the development of students' values was expressed by several superintendents. Within the schools there is a void of programs which foster patriotism, respect for law and order, acceptance of representative government, concern for mankind, and individual responsibility. To attack this problem, teacher training institutions must have additional programs, and total communities must become actively involved since the schools cannot do the job alone.

Before they can make significant changes in the curriculum, superintendents feel that the school districts must make greater provisions for a number of things which are now "scarce commodities" in the school organization. For example, teachers must have more time for planning and study; a greater number of consultation and coordinating services must be secured; material resources must be provided in greater abundance; and every district needs to allocate greater amounts of time and money to realistic in-service education programs for all professional personnel. Not the least of the needs for the improvement of the curriculum is increased community support, evidenced by both financial support and by constructive attitudes toward the schools' programs and professional educators.

Securing adequate curriculum resources and staffs is a problem of considerable magnitude for superintendents. Some school districts have limited or no facilities for instructional materials and no central libraries. One superintendent said, "We're without a facility to coordinate services and develop professional instructional materials. We have no research or information personnel. But we do have an athletic director!" A number of superintendents indicated that they have a resource staff but find them bogged down with special assignments and administrative details so that they do not exert a great deal of leadership.

Most of the instructional materials which are produced by commercial establishments are not oriented to the goals and needs of the local district. Exaggerated claims are frequently made for these materials (particularly technological devices) by manufacturers who publish data, presumably from respectable research sources, to attest to their effectiveness. But some of this research is inadequate and the conclusions are not justified. Local school districts generally do not have the specialized personnel and knowledge needed to evaluate the claims, and no other agency appears to be doing this for them. It is important that school districts have disinterested evaluations of new materials. It is also important that many resource materials be produced locally to meet local needs. This requires specialized staffs and considerable teacher time and leadership, both of which seem to be extremely limited.

The issues of time and resources raise a number of questions among superintendents: How do you justify the employment of more non-teaching personnel to the board and the community? When you get such personnel, how do you protect them from involvement in managerial chores to such an extent that they cannot give the leadership which is needed? How do you structure the teacher's day so he can devote time to planning and preparation? How do you free groups of teachers for sufficient periods of time to develop materials and programs? Can you expect teachers to engage in professional services to the school district after the school day ends for children? How do you get teachers to use wisely the planning time provided for them? How do you get teachers to use in their classrooms specialized assistance when it is provided for them?

Evaluation

The problem of evaluation raises a number of questions for superintendents: What is quality education? Who is to decide what is quality education? Should the professional educators alone establish the criteria? Or should citizens, parents, representatives of industry, and students themselves become involved?

Superintendents recognize that a great deal of "intuitive" evaluation is taking place, and the performance of students seems to be the major focus of measurement. It is very possible that, "we evaluate how kids perform on what might be poor programs. . . . We need to concentrate both on the evaluation of teaching and the evaluation of the effect of our teaching." A vast amount of testing of students has taken place in the schools using instruments developed by private companies. The selection of what is to be measured and the performance expectations are determined by these firms. It is questionable that the results of these tests reflect the results of a local school program upon the students. Also, there is little or no indication from these data as to what the program should be for a specific community. Some superintendents who encourage the involvement of lay people in evaluation find considerable resistance on the part of principals and teachers. It is felt that their resistance stems from teacher preparation programs which emphasize that the teacher or administrator is the professional, and lay people are "listeners, not tellers."

The evaluation of teaching is an area that presents many headaches for administrators. This problem is becoming more acute in light of legal provisions for tenure and recent negotiation procedures.

One desirable aspect of the present governmental programs has been the greater focus upon evaluation. Federal funds, with their accompanying requests for data to demonstrate the results of innovation and expanded programs, have in many instances caught educators "in their shorts." This emphasis upon evaluation has created problems and has caused superintendents to look for available resources. One superintendent put it this way:

I am not convinced that we know as much about basic education as we should. Too often programs are considered to be "good" because they have always been considered good. But, there is no logical basis for evaluating these programs.

Administrators, finding themselves unable to solve these problems alone, look to state departments of education or university staff members for assistance. There they find considerable variation in competencies, and many times they feel their own staff has greater competency.

Superintendents expressed a need for more relevant research data which have been carefully gathered, and written in a form that they can readily understand. There were a number of criticisms of past research conducted by universities, such as: (1) there is too much basic research and not enough action research; (2) present studies are written in such a way that they are not translatable to the practical problems of the district; and (3) developmental programs should replace some of the research that is being conducted.

In-service education

The development of planned programs of professional growth for all staff, particularly those who occupy administrative positions, is of concern to the majority of superintendents. Districts have conducted workshops and orientation programs for new teachers and numerous curriculum studies, which some administrators felt lacked effectiveness. Consultants were obtained both from within the staff of the districts and from without, using selected faculty of the universities. Other superintendents indicated that there was evidence of resistance to growth within the staff itself.

This resistance seems to stem partially from the inadequate teacher training programs and partially from the lack of a professional attitude of many teachers. One superintendent indicated that:

> Most teachers do not live in the district. They have no incentive or desire to return to school. They have a bachelor's degree or master's degree, even though it was obtained 25 years ago, and they feel it is sufficient. Also, they are on tenure.

Limited financial resources were also considered barriers to the development of effective in-service programs. Some districts found it difficult to get teachers to participate in intensive in-service programs without payment for their time. Others planned continuous in-service activities throughout the year and provided blocks of time for these activities to take place during the school day. Also, they had found both adequate and inadequate consultant services from the state departments of education and universities in the area.

Administrative Leadership

Quality of leadership

One of the major problems discussed by a number of superintendents was the level of competence of administrators. They claim there are too many incompetent administrators operating schools and holding membership in administrators' associations. This lack of competence has been evidenced by: (1) not taking a stand on issues, (2) low *esprit de corps* within the school and community, (3) inadequate educational leadership in the community, (4) little courage and vision, and (5) poor organization on the job with many functioning by the "seat of their pants." Part of the problem is that administrators have been inadequately prepared and improperly screened, both in and out of the administrative training programs.

Little emphasis upon sociology, history, philosophy, political science and psychology is to be found in administrative training programs. Little is done in developing skill in establishing effective personal relationships. Many university professors are so far removed from the level of what is going on in actual practice that what they attempt to teach is of little value. Also, many of these professors are frustrated or unsuccessful administrators.

Numerous administrators became leaders by accident and not by design. Their training and experience has been focused upon teaching rather than educational leadership, and success as a teacher does not assure effectiveness as an administrator. Many teachers have become administrators directly without adequate training.

The problem of obtaining qualified superintendents was mentioned by several participants as an area of serious concern. Unfortunately, many university placement bureaus and department staff members support superintendents who are constantly failing on the job. An evaluation of administrative performance seems to be lacking within the placement process. Consideration should be given the qualifications essential for successful performance in a unique assignment. It is possible that a superintendent, considering his specific education, experience, and personal qualifications, would be more successful in one situation than in another. The demands of the situation need to be determined and matched with the qualities of the candidate. There was some concern as to whether or not administrators in large cities need to have the personal experience of growing up in cities to become effective administrators in them. Not much is known about the relationship of prior experiences to successful on-the-job performance of administrators.

Much more attention also should be accorded to the recruitment process. Some superintendents feel that there are still too many jobs in administration filled by former coaches and bandmasters. Entry into the first administrative job is frequently determined on the basis of political considerations rather than on soundly assessed potential for success as an administrator. Techniques need to be established for identifying candidates with high potential for success in administration, and individuals so identified should be provided some initial opportunities to test their interest in administrative careers. No one mentioned the question of admitting women to administrative careers, but then, the entire sample did consist of men!

There should be a design for preparing administrators in the future. This design should include: (1) recruitment of top quality people; (2) an organized screening process upon entry into the program, during the preparation period, and after the administrator is placed on the job; (3) a strong training program taught by a quality staff; and (4) an internship program to give trainees needed experience. Close cooperation between local school districts and institutions of higher learning is needed to develop adequate programs. Salary schedules must be improved to attract and hold quality people and to compete with industry.

Trying to keep up professionally with recent research and developments was a problem expressed by the majority of superintendents. A lack of time seemed to be the most frequently stated reason for falling behind. The major portion of the administrator's time is spent dealing with problems of finances and in meetings with members of the staff and community. Several superintendents indicated that their time possibly could be organized more efficiently, and some of the things they are presently doing delegated to other personnel. Some conceded that they are frequently criticized for failure to delegate, but the problem is not that simple. Subordinates, too, have time-allocation problems, and the superintendent has to protect them from getting involved in too many routine chores. There seems to be an "innate antagonism" of school board members and citizens to the employment of subordinate administrators to relieve superintendents of routine responsibilities. Superintendents frequently hear the old cliché, "too many chiefs and not enough Indians," and fear that requests for more assistants will destroy their conservative image. As a result they recommend additional assistants only as a last resort.

A need was expressed for more in-service programs for superintendents for which top level consultants could be brought into a region for a series of workshops. It was suggested that possibly USOE could organize such programs and secure the best consultants available. Strengthening the leadership of the public schools would be the best investment the federal government could make toward the improvement of education. Without effective, dynamic leadership the whole system will continue to move at "glacial speed."

Political involvement

Two points of view were expressed regarding educators' involvement in the political arena. The dominant view is that superintendents should play a leadership role in many organizations in order to reach the influentials in the community. Since the superintendent is primarily responsible for obtaining financial support for the schools and developing favorable attitudes within the community, much of his time is spent in political activities, whether or not he likes to admit it. Expressing this point of view, a superintendent stated:

> Every district in the nation is involved in politics. The existence of the school is dependent upon political action. The public school is an arm of the state, and administrators need to become involved in politics. The board knows that I tell the faculty what each candidate stands for. They also know that if a candidate is for education, then I'm for him; if he is not for education, then I'm against him.

Inevitably, the superintendent manipulates and influences people. Superintendents should be encouraged to learn from management what is effective and what are the concepts and the techniques of manipulation. These concepts and skills should be included in administrative training programs.

The second point of view is more conservative, proposing that if a superintendent engages in political activity, he should be nonpartisan. The question was raised, "What happens to the superintendent if he backs one candidate and the other is elected?" The superintendent can place the school district in jeopardy because of his political activities.

In a few districts, when teachers have become actively involved in political affairs it has created difficult problems. Requests have been brought before the board by teachers asking for leaves of absence with full pay while they serve in the legislature. Teachers' associations have taken an active stand in the election of board members, and this action has aroused considerable public opposition.

Board-superintendent relations

Much concern was expressed regarding the quality of local board members and the task of indoctrinating them to become effective participants. Several superintendents indicated that recently board membership has tended to shift from professional type persons to hack politicians, racists, or housewives "with an axe to grind." At present there are very few communities which have established legal qualifications for board membership or which practice informal screening of board candidates. A suggestion was made that the state department of education should establish qualifications for prospective board members and that a local committee, composed of local residents, be formed to screen candidates. Each year, in most districts, the superintendent is faced with a board of varied composition, purposes, and knowledge about the operation of schools.

For board members to function adequately and understand their roles in relationship to the superintendent, the professional staff, and the community, a planned program of education and training must be carried out. This, again, requires time, which the superintendent finds to be a scarce commodity, and he must rely upon other resources of varying degrees of effectiveness which he finds available. The state and national school board associations provide some in-service opportunities, and many state departments of education conduct workshops and conferences for board members.

Superintendents have experienced both positive and negative effects as a result of board members' participation in these kinds of activities. Some board members have become enlightened and knowledgeable in the new technology of modern education and, as a result, have tended to involve themselves in the executive phases of school district administration. Other board members, with an "axe to grind," have attended workshops and, upon return, have left their "axes" behind! In general, the superintendents consider the in-service and workshop activities to have a positive influence toward developing more effective board members. Many times board members thought they knew more about educational administration than the professionals, and much of the time they were right. One superintendent commented:

> My board is composed of a scientist, a corporation administrator, a millionaire, and a college professor. This is one of the most difficult boards I have had to work with. Many of the problems which arise in the district go directly to the individual board member rather than to the superintendent or other professional staff. It takes considerable work to get

them to refer these problems to the professional staff rather than to handle them directly themselves.

Other superintendents agreed that this communication problem was one experienced by many of them.

Popular magazines have recently contained articles quoting, or misquoting, leading educators regarding the diminishing importance of the local school board. These articles have created considerable conflict as board members have felt compelled, because of these comments, to become increasingly involved in administration to justify their existence. Superintendents in the sample disagreed on whether or not the role of local school boards was decreasing in importance. Some felt that the board's role is changing as society is changing. Others considered the role to be the same, namely, that of a policy and decision-making body, but that problems with which they are confronted in a changing society are different.

Several superintendents indicated that the most important function of the local school board is the hiring of the best superintendent available. Unfortunately most boards don't know how to find a good administrator, nor do they know how to evaluate one after they get him. Board members generally base their decisions upon incidental information or biases. It was proposed that assistance could be rendered by a screening committee, composed of practicing superintendents, professors from colleges and universities, teachers, and possibly a personnel manager of a corporation. This committee would interview the candidates, describe and evaluate their qualifications for the position, and pass on the information to the local board. The board members then could make the final choice for their community. This assistance would also facilitate the evaluation process after the superintendent is employed.

Board members should not be trained to administer a school district, but should be informed about the diversity and the complexity of the operation. They should be helped to recognize the importance of a highly trained staff, and they should be taught how to evaluate a superintendent. This is an ongoing educative process involving staff members, other superintendents, old board members, and university consultants.

The role of the superintendent

Many superintendents indicated that one of their greatest problems is attempting to define their role as a school superintendent.

In the smaller districts, superintendents tend to consider themselves the educational leader and take pride in maintaining individual contact with all the teachers in the district. They know what is happening in all schools in the district and are a direct source of information for the staff, the board, and the community.

In larger districts, the superintendent finds that he does not have the time for all of these functions. Here, superintendents perceive themselves in diverse roles depending upon their philosophy of leadership and the expectations of the board. Many superintendents consider their role primarily as a leader of numerous specialists who have been delegated responsibilities according to their positions. In such cases, the job of the superintendent becomes one of stimulator of change by selling, influencing, and politically manipulating others. Other superintendents accept the managerial role and operate within the structure of a bureaucratic organization. Communications are from the top down; regulations are numerous; and relationships are distant.

One superintendent indicated that his role was not so much that of a manager or educational leader, as that of a facilitator of group action. The district educational council, composed of representatives of the professional staff, provided the leadership and made the decisions affecting the educational program in the school. The people who made the decisions were those involved in implementing them. As a superintendent, his role was to provide the opportunities for decisions to be made by the appropriate groups.

A few superintendents of the large districts attempt to maintain the role of educational leader, but find themselves involved in more pressing societal issues. In fact, superintendents generally feel that they are spending an increasing amount of time in community affairs. In the past, the superintendent's leadership was not sought out by community organizations. Recently, however, community officials are asking schoolmen for assistance in cooperative planning. Many superintendents are now becoming concerned that their community obligations are restricting their availability to the school staff.

Communications and human relations

One of the biggest problems for many superintendents is maintaining good human relations within both the organization and the community. As one superintendent put it, "Almost everyone who comes to the superintendent's office has a problem of some kind. Our ability to handle them largely determines our success as administrators." Yet, many administrators admit they lack skill and confidence in their ability to deal effectively with people. They indicated that their training did not prepare them adequately in this area. Something needs to be done in order to provide them assistance and fill in the gaps which so obviously exist.

Concern was expressed regarding the public's growing lack of faith in educators. Much is written in the news media about ineffective teachers, poor methods, financial waste, and so on. This barrage of criticism has led parents to wonder about what is happening to their children in their schools. Broad generalizations are made about what is going on in schools today, and people tend to believe what they want to believe. "Blind trust in the educator is gone." No longer can educators speak about education as though they were talking about "motherhood and chastity." The public is asking for evidence about the results of existing educational programs. They want facts and hard proof, not the traditional, glittering generalities. This attitude presents real problems to administrators as their evaluation instruments are weak and their channels of communication uncertain.

Communications within the organization of a district present many problems for superintendents. In large districts, the superintendent doesn't even get to know all the principals or his central office staff. Through breakfast meetings, luncheons, advisory committees, study committees, and school visitations the superintendent has attempted to become at least visible to administrators and staff. Verbal and written communications are constantly distorted as they are transmitted throughout the organization.

How to identify the various publics in a community and communicate with them is a problem which faces most of the superintendents in the sample. Little or no contact has been made with some segments of some communities, and, as a result, superintendents fear that these people are alienated from the schools. They characteristically do not vote in school elections, but when they do, they are generally negative on financial measures. As one superintendent put it:

> We can communicate reasonably well with the economic power structure of the community, which has been demonstrated by favorable response to past bond elections. There is a large mass of individuals, not the power structure and not the disadvantaged, that we have difficulty reaching. I don't know if we communicate with them at all.

Several superintendents indicated that their districts have moved in so many directions at such a rate of speed that it has not been possible to keep the community informed. Now they are concerned that misunderstandings are developing, and loss of community support may ensue. A bit of advice was offered by another superintendent who stated, "The key to support for schools is honesty, openness, and involvement of the public."

There are particular problems of public relations in the inner city where school officials must communicate with individuals who are illiterate and have few educational aspirations for their children. Human relations departments have been established by several districts specifically for the purpose of attempting to service the needs of these people. The problems which these departments face are extremely difficult and are so numerous that to provide adequate staff to handle the situation is beyond the present means of the district.

Administrative organization

A central issue for many superintendents of the larger districts is the development of a decentralized administrative structure which enables decisions to be made as close to the operating level as possible. The question superintendents raised was, "In what size city and under what circumstances should a school district decentralize its administration by the appointment of area superintendents or directors?"

Cities of any size have diversified needs, and decentralization makes it possible for an area superintendent to work directly with a staff to develop the instructional adaptations appropriate to his area. There are many problems inherent in this type of decentralization, one of which is to determine whether or not there should be a duplication of resource personnel in each of the component areas. Should it be a duplication of present central office staff? Another concern involves the problems of communication which arise from this decentralization. The area superintendents become a buffer between the local schools and the central office. The general superintendent becomes the "man in waiting," as he can't go out to get information first hand, but must acquire it through the area superintendents. There is danger of excessive fragmentation, as each area may consider itself an independent system rather than a segment of a unified district with an overall policy. The district superintendent, too, may consider only the local area as his reference group and build pressures upon the superintendent and school board to gain special consideration for his area.

Many superintendents from various sized school districts were concerned about how to organize and staff the central office to provide effective services for all schools. Traditional patterns of organization have not been highly effective, and they lead to too much fragmentation, particularly at the elementary school level. Except for a few creative attempts, no sound models worthy of emulation appear to have been established.

There is also fear of the staff becoming so large that the superintendent is effectively isolated from it. One superintendent told of an administrative assistant who moved about the district, giving directives as though they came from the superintendent and creating a very unfavorable image of the superintendent. In a large number of school systems today the superintendent must speak to many staff members through his representatives, but he realizes that they might not always report his point of view to best advantage or sustain his favorable image. In some instances, the only solution to such problems of communication may be the constant restructuring of the roles of central office personnel, but superintendents recognize that this solution inevitably leads to insecurity and ineffectiveness of operations.

Superintendents generally acknowledged that central offices were understaffed and that their districts did not provide the materials necessary to maintain an entirely adequate educational program. In some instances, they felt that their salary schedules did not enable them to buy the consultative services of highly skilled specialists.

One of their more critical concerns, however, was that they lacked the resources to enable them to free teachers to work on the development of instructional materials or curricular programs. They said that at present teachers are scheduled so rigidly and are bogged down with so much paper work that they have little time for planning, evaluation, or developmental activities, let alone their own professional growth. Few have the opportunity for "setting their sights beyond the moment-to-moment activities of the day." This insufficiency of personnel within the school organization promotes the "glacial climate" which freezes the system. Periodically, pilot programs were instituted and found to be beneficial to students. However, when the attempts were made to implement the program district-wide, the plan failed and the program died out. There was obviously insufficient organization for program development and implementation within the district. Superintendents indicate that they would like to know what organizational pattern will facilitate getting the job done and what measures are needed to "thaw out" the system.

Decision-making

A problem confronting every superintendent is that of obtaining adequate information upon which to base his decisions. This problem was mentioned in relation to all phases of school administration, and particularly to the overall problems of negotiating with staff, evaluating the curriculum, recruiting teachers, and advising the board. Many decisions are made on the basis of fuzzy generalizations rather than facts. Superintendents feel that there is a great deal of data available, but they do not have the time or personnel needed to review and organize it so it is usable in their decision-making. Some superintendents hope the situation can be improved through the use of electronic data processing equipment. Several have had an extensive management study of their system and are about to reorganize and further implement information services.

For many administrators this is an age of pressure groups. At board meetings, groups present problems based upon data which they have previously gathered and press for immediate board action. There is neither time nor resources available to most districts for the superintendent to analyze adequately and evaluate carefully their claims and demands. Yet, he is frequently made to answer these groups without adequate preparation and is put in a very awkward position before the board and the public.

One superintendent found that role-playing board meetings with the administrative staff previous to board sessions was helpful in determining what additional data may be necessary for making decisions. It was also suggested that better decisions resulted from group discussion than from individual contemplation and hunch. But these are time-consuming techniques and interfere with the staff's performance of routine responsibilities.

A superintendent, thinking aloud about questions which required answers based upon valid information presently unavailable, asked:

> How do I structure the organizational pattern to get the job done? How do you organize and run a good personnel department? What services do you perform for colleges to assist them to do their job? What type of teachers do you want in your district? What follow-up is necessary in order to determine how well your teachers are doing? How are teachers assigned in order to use their strengths? How do you get principals involved in policy making? How do you evaluate teachers accurately? How can you build self-esteem in teachers? Are our methods of evaluating ourselves honest? Should teachers evaluate principals? How do you handle complaints? What is the legal authority for dismissal? Do we need a special department for handling federal programs and implementing them?

He said these were but a few of the areas he would like to have researched for him.

Several participants discussed in some detail the need for their obtaining greater understanding and skill in decision-making. Several indicated that some administrators appear to "lose courage" after a number of years in office and need to be revitalized. Others found themselves lacking decision-making skill from the beginning. Suggestions were made for sensitivity and group dynamic training institutes, simulation workshops, and other in-service type programs which should be provided by universities or state departments of education.

Critical Social Issues

Racial problems

Most superintendents are frustrated by the racial problems which confront them. Many of them are not fully convinced that it is the job of the school to attempt to remedy societal problems. They face the tasks and the conflicts with mixed emotions largely because they lack confidence in the ability of the schools to accomplish the objectives that have been set for them. Most superintendents have not been able to solve the dilemma of how to proceed most effectively to meet the educational problems produced by either *de facto* segregation or dual school systems.

The problems involved are varied. The problem of faculty and staff assignment looms as one of the most important to superintendents. In or near areas with large Negro populations, it is difficult to keep a school faculty from becoming entirely Negro. Few qualified white teachers want to teach in these schools, and there is a constant pressure from the best white and Negro teachers for transfers into neighborhoods which do not have so many pressing problems. However, Negro teachers are frequently isolated and lonely when assigned to teach among almost all white teachers.

A major problem faced by many superintendents as they attack the problems of integration is that of locating qualified personnel. "There just aren't enough qualified Negro teachers available." Nor are there enough white teachers who understand and can work effectively with the cultural problems associated with disadvantaged children and youth. Most teachers have come from middle class backgrounds and have accepted educational values of the middle class. They do not understand, nor are they in sympathy with, significantly different points of view. Superintendents point out that teachers have always had difficulty understanding children who lacked motivation for school accomplishment, and in the large urban cities where the problems of minority groups and lower class children are so acute, their failures to deal with these children effectively amount to a serious crisis.

In spite of the staffing problems involved, comments indicate that a considerable amount of progress has been made in staff desegregation. Negro principals and teachers are now frequently seen on previously all-white staffs, and white principals and teachers are no longer entirely absent from previously all-Negro staffs. Major problems have arisen in districts which were "formed to keep the youth away from the Negro elements," but even here some Negro teachers are now being hired, even though no local lodging could be found.

Policy decisions relative to qualifications for employment must be carefully considered for racial inequities. For instance, the National Teachers' Examination scores were found to be discriminatory toward Negro teachers when they were used as a salary criterion. In some areas of the country, Negro teachers have not received training equal to that of some of their white colleagues. They were forced to attend Negro training institutions whose staffs had graduated from Negro colleges and whose standards were lower than those of comparable white institutions. Consequently, an instrument such as the National Teachers' Examination can be used, and already is being used, as a powerful means of discrimination against Negro teachers.

Practically all superintendents agreed that if both administrative and teaching staffs are fully integrated, racial problems can be dealt with more effectively. This approach is recognized as one which greatly facilitates communication between racial groups on school problems.

Some of the other problems are no less significant. What kinds of programs should the school provide for the Negro student in the predominantly white schools and *vice versa?* What kinds of records should be kept of racial data for reports to the USOE and other groups? What is going to happen when the racial groups start looking toward control of the schools? How do you involve minority groups in the decision-making structure of the schools? How do you deal with the politically-oriented leadership of civil rights groups? How do you maintain rapport with the homes in disadvantaged neighborhoods? How does the superintendent deal with politicians in the community who would use the school for their own ends, regardless of the significance for education?

Some superintendents said that the fact that some communities "don't have immediate problems facing them in the area of segregation" does not mean that they aren't a part of the total problem of the desegregation of public schools. Districts with no immediate desegregation problems may receive migrations of families from surrounding districts that do have such problems. The superintendent of such a district says, "We are part of society and we have to shoulder responsibilities for helping to find solutions and even involving our own school districts in helping to find solutions." Unless the district which is "free of segregation problems" assumes some responsibility, it "just isn't going to be possible for neighboring school districts to accomplish the necessary objectives." He doubts, however, that his school board and most of the members of the community share his views and his readiness to use the district as a means of helping to solve the problem which exists among their neighbors.

Directly related to these comments was the statement by another superintendent of a "completely integrated" district that this integration might be "in name only." He has noticed that "Negro children are much by themselves on the playground."

Superintendents have implemented a variety of techniques in attempting to meet racial problems. Busing is a common attempt to begin integration procedures. The results of busing have been mixed. It was ruled illegal in one state; in one district it was found ineffective; in a third district it was considered effective as part of a program aimed at integration. Urban renewal exerts a strong influence for integration for a time, but in some cases population migrations negated the positive effects after a short time.

Changes in attendance regulations to allow more flexibility for the student have been found effective. Freedom-of-choice plans are fairly common and evidently have been appraised as successful in some districts. In spite of their success in some places, the freedom-of-choice plans are only temporary measures, according to some superintendents. They impose extra transportation upon Negro pupils, and few, if any, white pupils elect to attend Negro schools. Genuine compensatory education is essential, and efforts must be made to provide the resources needed for such programs. Some superintendents say they feel a need to do this even at the risk of taking resources now allocated to schools in more fortunate neighborhoods.

The educational plaza is another attempt, in part, to eliminate racial problems. In one Eastern district such a plaza has been designed to accommodate 10,000 students. The plaza is not yet completely finished, but resistance is strong from many quarters. While there appears to be no question that the Negro-white balance would be improved, "many community members do not want integration to this extent."

A number of superintendents feel that they have facilitated integration when they have directed attention toward purely educational solutions rather than the problem of racial balance itself. Less community resistance, they feel, is encountered when a school is closed because of its "limited curriculum" rather than because it is "segregated." Superintendents generally feel that educational solutions are the only realistic approach to the problem. "We have wasted too much time," they say, "on what amounts to political solutions. Now we need to invest time and money to find desirable educational techniques which will bring relief to the situation."

Organizing the staff to handle intercultural relations effectively is a difficult process. There is a basic organizational question as to "whether this is a responsibility which should be handled by all administrative personnel or centrally located in a single office." The problem appears to be that if this responsibility is located in a single office, other people abrogate their responsibilities and depend too much on the office. The department becomes a symbol of district policy, but frequently it is a center of controversy. If it is successful, it arouses the resentment of those who have not been able to deal effectively with inter-cultural problems. If it is not successful, it is criticized because it has not brought relief to other administrators who have unsolved problems of group relations.

In some areas community resistance runs strongly against attempts to eliminate segregation, whether *de facto* or legislated. It appears that when a school reaches a certain percentage of Negro students, a point called "the tipping point" in the South, the remaining white families move to the suburbs and the school becomes all Negro. In some instances, a slow movement to integrate previously all-white neighborhoods proceeded satisfactorily until Negro families moved into the neighborhoods, following the admission of their children to the neighborhood schools. As the proportion of Negroes in the schools reached about 30 percent, the rates of white *em*igration and Negro *im*migration rapidly accelerated. Rather significant attempts at desegregation resulted in a "*re*segregation" of the schools.

Speaking very frankly, one superintendent rationalized about this problem. He said that in his district, the program provided for Negro students is not as "academically respectable" as that for predominantly white students. There is a variety of reasons for this which the schools have been unable to avoid; but the fact remains that white parents who leave their children in schools which have an increasing Negro population run the risk of their getting an inferior education. This fact is not related to the academic abilities of the Negro students or teachers. It arises from the white power structure's continuing neglect of the Negro community and its schools and the failure to make provisions which take into consideration the unique needs of these schools. As one administrator said, the general policy of the district is to provide one teacher for 35 children, but in the areas in which there is an increasing Negro and declining white enrollment, the educational problems are such that there should not be more than 15 or 20 children in a single classroom. Yet, the school board will not make exceptions to the general standards of the district.

Communication is difficult. One superintendent pointed out that in his district, community organizations such as the PTA were once available to him for direct communication about the schools. However, this was largely a middle class group of white parents. These people have now migrated to the suburbs, the city is over 70 percent Negro, and the superintendent feels he has no groups with which to communicate. He wants to find the means to establish communication with these new citizens, but he has found the groups with which they are affiliated "extremely jealous and suspicious of each other."

Superintendents report that they have some unique difficulties in dealing with the Negro community. They find it very difficult to "identify the power structure in the Negro community." Typically there are several young men "competing for power." One man will be in the key position for a few days or weeks, and then he loses his status to someone else. This is one of the difficulties which superintendents are encountering in their relationships with community action groups in the Negro neighborhoods. Failure to stabilize the leadership in the Negro community means not only instability of personal relationships but insecurity for any programs which are established with their cooperation.

In spite of some criticism, there is general agreement that the effects of federal guidelines on integration have been beneficial. Without the pressure of these guidelines, progress would be much slower. At the same time, however, one superintendent who seemed very positive toward the intent of the guidelines stated that he felt that they went too far. The guidelines are "pitched so strongly to people who resist that those who are trying to do the job find they encounter barriers."

An unusual situation is being faced by the superintendent of one large southern district. The schools in his state are completely under the state authority and the state has indicated that "federal guidelines are null and void." The governor and the state superintendent of education agree on this at the present time, which "presents a considerable problem." The state superintendent has offered more school support to districts which will "maintain segregated schools." This puts the local district superintendent "right in the middle." The federal courts have ordered his district to integrate while there is strong political pressure from the highest state officials to resist.

A potentially serious problem regarding segregation and federal aid to education was raised by superintendents in the East. It appears to them that to the extent that federal aid is expended to private and parochial schools irrespective of their integrated statuses, segregation is being encouraged. "The more segregation is pushed, the more parochial school enrollment is increased, creating segregation of another type." In one large Eastern metropolis, the parochial schools constitute 39 per cent of the total school enrollment of the district, but less than 15 percent of their enrollment is non-white. More than 60 percent of the school enrollment in the public schools is non-white. The white retreat from desegregation is not only to the suburbs but also to the parochial and private schools. There is some feeling that while the federal government operates under the child benefit theory, it is helping to encourage segregation in the North, while attempting to eliminate it in the South.

Cultural deprivation

Educating the culturally deprived child presents special problems for superintendents. Partly racial but largely economic, this problem is again a societal issue with which the school must deal. There are large numbers of families who feel trapped in the urban centers. Typical problems mentioned include: It is not unusual for well over half of these parents to be illiterate. When the school sends a form home to these parents, it is "lucky to receive a ten percent return." The parents couldn't fill out these forms even if they wanted to. Gang warfare is a reality in the severely deprived areas, and the superintendent may sometimes use the leadership of the most powerful gangs to help maintain discipline by appointing them as monitors in the halls. City-wide teacher-pupil ratios are applied to the deprived areas, and they are much too high for effective teaching. Teachers lack an understanding of the values and motivations of these children.

Qualified teachers of the culturally deprived are difficult to locate.

Administrators try to get their best teachers to work in the schools of the culturally deprived neighborhoods, but in actual fact, "the teachers in these areas are usually a little less than average." One superintendent said that the teachers who score in the lowest quarter of the National Teachers' Examination are the ones who are willing to teach in the disadvantaged and/or minority race areas.

One of the factors which results in the shortage of staff in the disadvantaged areas is that the teacher has to "take more responsibility for the youngsters than is true in the schools with average, middle class students." Students new to the urban areas especially are in need of extra help. In these schools the normal chores, such as playground or hall duty, are focal points of unrest and violent disturbance. Teachers read the newspaper reports about these difficulties in inner core schools and refuse to teach in them.

In attempting to meet the needs of these groups, the schools have tried a variety of programs. The pupil-teacher ratio has been reduced from 34:1 to 24:1 throughout the elementary schools of one district and to a ratio of 18:1 in the most disadvantaged areas. Job skill training programs which have been implemented at the secondary level are "geared to the problems which occur on the job."

No real indication was given regarding the degree of satisfaction or dissatisfaction with these programs. However, the superintendent of a district in which 500 young people per year return from penal institutions stated that "it seems that the solution to this problem is beyond our resources at the present time." It appears that no adequate solution has yet been discovered for the problem of educating the severely disadvantaged youth.

Religion

The problems of church-state relations are far from resolved in education. This is particularly true in the East, and to a slightly lesser degree in the southern part of the Midwest. Since many communities are frequently polarized around religious issues, the superintendent feels extremely uncomfortable and insecure in dealing with these problems.

The question of religious holidays presents difficulties. The minimum number of school days per year is legally prescribed. Yet students and teachers may legally have the right to be excused for religious holidays. The superintendent must then attempt to "get in the legally required minimum" between the various holidays. One Midwestern superintendent fears that the proliferation of religious sects, each with individual holidays, may eventually result in the closing of schools for all religious holidays. The feeling expressed is that religious observances are interfering unnecessarily with the children's school attendance.

The presence of one or more strong religious groups in a district may present unique educational problems. In a community which is one-third Jewish, one-third Catholic, and one-third Protestant, the Jewish people have a group which informs Jewish board members of their wishes. When the mayor considers appointments to the school board, "it is open fact that he goes to the Monsignor for recommendations." Consequently, "the Monsignor directs the interests of education through the school board members in the county." There is no real spokesman for the Protestant group. As a result, Catholic school facilities are reputedly "much better than public school facilities," with carpeted classrooms and television sets in each room.

In another community the citizens are split between Catholic and Jewish religions. The school program has as one of its objectives "the helping of all to understand one another." Yet, the Jewish parents say that the Catholics are trying to introduce the church into school affairs, and the Catholics say "The Jews are trying to run everything." The board consists of four Jewish members and one Catholic. On such matters as the "textbook loan law," the board "cannot cenceive of its motivation being educational rather than religious."

There is also concern for other issues, such as prayer in the schools, shared facilities, released time, textbooks and transportation. In the East, religious groups are particularly concerned with the political affairs of the school districts. In the so-called "Bible-belt," there is more concern about the elimination of prayer and the use of school facilities and resources for minority religious groups.

Extremism

Conspicuous by its absence was the topic of extremism. The literature relating to problems of the superintendency indicated that extremism and dealing with extremist groups are serious problems. Yet, only one superintendent referred to this issue. He stated that the John Birch Society is particularly difficult to fight because "they come out strongly for motherhood, country, and so on."

It appears that if extremism is of concern to superintendents at all, it is either a secondary problem or one which superintendents did not wish to discuss.

Finance

Financial responsibilities of superintendents

Financing the schools is a major problem mentioned by the superintendents, and several of them listed it as their single most important problem. Most districts suffer from a lack of balance in school support from local, state, and federal governments and, according to a large number of the superintendents, local responsibility is much too heavily emphasized. The problem is particularly acute in financing capital outlay, and it is not uncommon for a district to be bonded to total capacity, to have exhausted every legal resource for raising additional money, and still not have enough money to build needed schools. With rapidly increasing school budgets, superintendents feel that money is becoming much more difficult to obtain.

Superintendents believe that they are constantly spending more of their time and energy on financial problems. As one superintendent stated, "Finance is always a big problem and most of the superintendent's time is spent in this area. The total program is structured on the basis of available resources."

Superintendents also feel the pressure of time from their involvement in obtaining funds. In a financial campaign one superintendent made 37 major addresses in a two-week period. Often the superintendent considers himself to be a financier rather than an educational leader. District policy is influenced by finance in many ways. Boards and communities are inclined to assess programs more on their costs than on educational values, and no proposal can be viewed apart from its financial implications.

Within the general area of school finance, several specific problem areas were mentioned. One superintendent mentioned that in his state the equalization formula for transportation was not fair and his district suffers from it. Another superintendent mentioned that school district reorganization is impeded because smaller districts fear their taxes will increase. The board in another district is reluctant to set aside a percentage of the budget for money to stimulate change and research within the district. Special services are difficult to finance, and although people seem to want the best, they aren't willing to pay the taxes that will buy the best.

Suburbia is in a critical position with regard to finance. The state has been using money from the industrial central-city areas to support the non-industrial suburban areas. However, the central city now has increasing financial needs, and funds are no longer available to support education in suburbia.

One superintendent feels that financial problems are created by the superintendent himself. It is unfair and unwise for a superintendent to compare his district to others throughout the country. He must, instead, "investigate his own local resources and operate on the basis of what he can afford." Superintendents must learn to be "more practical" and must not sell to a district an educational program which it cannot afford. Superintendents were, however, sharply divided on this issue. Some felt that it was their responsibility to educate the board and citizens to the ways quality can be constantly increased. They felt that any community could support a level of education which it truly wanted. Others felt it was wrong for a superintendent to try to sell a program which would be difficult to support and maintain.

Taxation

Wherever the property tax is the primary source of financial support for education, superintendents feel that legislative changes are necessary. "People are fed up with the real estate tax." In many states, the property assessment level is set by law, and the citizens are opposed to increasing that level, even though the schools are in financial difficulties. Tax assessors may be appointed by state officials, and there is some suspicion that political factors may affect the equality of assessments. In addition, there is increasing competition for the limited supply of tax dollars.

Problems regarding the property tax appear to have many sources. For one thing, the property tax is not based on income. In some states some property has never been accurately assessed. Because of governmental activity much property is not on the tax rolls even though it produces enrollment for the schools. One school district, for instance, included a university, a mental hospital, and two naval bases, none of which was subject to property tax. Last year this district educated over 300 children of employees of the university with no tax dollars from that campus to help support the schools.

The local property tax is the one tax over which the local taxpayer can exert some direct control. People's feelings against taxes in general can be vented against the property tax because they are able "to do something about it." This puts all tax-supported agencies in a hazardous position.

Legislative control

In one state the schools receive money from the state in a variety of different categories. However, the amounts to be allocated in these various categories are not known until the legislature adjourns each year in June or July. This delayed action leaves the schools in the unfortunate position of being unsure of available resources until summer. The obvious budgetary problems engendered by such a procedure need no discussion.

Much of the superintendents' concern about financial problems centers around legislative matters. The composition of the legislature in several states, for instance, has been largely rural. For the superintendent in a large city, the rurally oriented and dominated legislature has been a definite disadvantage. Formulas for the distribution of state funds to schools have given disproportionate consideration to rural areas to the neglect of the cities. Legislatures are frequently dominated by the financial conservatism of rural areas, and this is one reason the states have not provided more money for education.

The formulas used by various states for the distribution of state funds are established by the legislature. Many superintendents felt that distribution formulas are inequitable and obsolete. One district has a high population of transient students, most of whom are in attendance for only a short time when school opens in the fall. However, since state funds are allocated on the basis of average daily attendance, this leaves the school with insufficient funds to cover equipment, materials, and books needed to care for the maximum of students in attendance during the year. For a variety of reasons, city superintendents feel that the urban school districts in rurally dominated states need more state funds than normally allocated to the rural districts. Urban superintendents feel that the states need to become more aware of urban school problems and needs.

Most superintendents contend that the only satisfactory solutions to financial problems of education must come from the state legislature. It is the only agency which can do something to ease the burdens of the local taxpayer, through changing the tax structure or finding sources of new revenue. Superintendents, board members, and legislators must communicate with one another to find solutions to the problems.

Federal aid

Several superintendents feel that the federal government must also be involved in financing education. "The federal government has to get into this. Their collection methods are the most efficient and the fairest we have come up with." The support appears to be for grants directly to the states rather than for categorical aid. There could be "some equalization support from the federal government to the states according to their ability to support their schools." As it is desirable for the states to finance the basic program, the federal government should make grants only directly to the states. Many of the superintendents fear that legislatures will not fully cooperate with the federal government since they are concerned with federal control and represent "vested interests which are opposed to any extension of the income tax."

Probably the greatest problem which federal financing of school programs poses for superintendents is the system of fund allocations. Superintendents complained that federal programs are supported "on a hand-to-mouth" basis. The USOE can authorize programs and allocate funds only after Congress has appropriated them. Congress works on no schedule, and funds have been appropriated annually at times which have no relation to the academic year. Superintendents also realize that for succeeding years Congress can undo all that this year's session accomplished. If the federal government is to play a role as a persistent partner in the financing of education, superintendents feel that it must stabilize funds and programs which permit long range planning.

Community control

Some superintendents feel that the primary cause of the financial problems lies in community control and the fact that people must either vote on school district budgets or the tax levy to provide funds for them. They state that the county, city, and state simply "levy taxes for increases in funds which they find necessary." Consequently, they wonder if the schools would also not be better managed if the citizens of the local community did not have to vote on school levies. The superintendent of a fiscally dependent school district stated that he felt his school district has more adequate funds under the system where the board of aldermen approved the budget and levied the tax, since, under this system, the "tendency is to provide the resources which the school needs." Other superintendents from fiscally dependent districts felt that much of the popular pressure was taken off them, and they found minimal difficulties in working with governing bodies of their municipalities.

Obtaining resources for teachers' salaries and school buildings appears to be the most serious and continuous financial problem for superintendents. Since teachers' salaries constitute up to 80 percent of the district's annual budget, increases in teachers' salaries are the primary reason for large budgetary increments. When school boards raise teachers' salaries, there is always a great deal of publicity in the press. Now that salaries are generally above the average salaries of the community, citizens compare the presumed nine months' salary of teachers against their own, and resentment is frequently aroused.

There is also reluctance to allocate funds to the capital budget for construction purposes. One superintendent stated that in his district new buildings are non-existent; additions and renovations to old buildings have been the pattern for years. In one large metropolitan district, the superintendent sees the need for 90 million dollars in new capital construction. Several school buildings in that district are over 50 years old and at least one is over 100 years old. At least a fourth of the school buildings in this district are "unfit for school." Yet, in the upcoming bond election the board is asking for only 25 million dollars.

Perhaps educational leaders themselves are to blame for the difficulty in obtaining resources for salaries and buildings. One superintendent says, "We don't have the courage to go for what would really do the job that needs to be done with regard to salaries." And the superintendent in the metropolitan district discussed above says that the 25 million dollar bond election has been sold to the public only because it's "a pittance."

Summary

These were the problems which superintendents identified. Insofar as possible, we used their own words and their own ways of identifying the issues. The ways in which the problems are categorized is the responsibility of the researchers. A fuller analysis of the implications and significance of how superintendents view their problems will be reserved for the final chapter. It is noteworthy at this point, however, that the problems appear to arise from relatively few sources. They arise from the major social dislocations affecting American society; from the rapid social changes affecting American communities which impose changes upon the schools; from cultural changes which necessitate new role definitions for educational administrators; from individual characteristics of superintendents; and seemingly, from the persistence of traditional modes of organizational behavior and governmental structures and practices.

Faced with the myriad tasks and responsibilities of operating his schools, except for special occasions, the superintendent has little opportunity to study his problems carefully and in their fullest context. As was frequently mentioned, the superintendent has to work with the tools he can find—he lacks the time to create the new tools which may be needed. The following chapters will deal with the agencies from which he hopes these tools will emerge.

3/

The U. S. Office of Education
and Its Services
to Superintendents

The Changing Role and Characteristics of USOE

Historical background

Possibly no agency of government has experienced more rapid and fundamental change in its structure and functions than the United States Office of Education. Established in 1867 in an era when public education was a matter of local concern and did not occupy a great deal of national attention, the Federal Department of Education (now USOE) was expected to do only a limited job in a narrowly circumscribed way. Official and public expectations for its performance were slight and easily met. Its mission was to collect "statistics and facts showing the condition and progress of education, and to diffuse such information as shall aid the people of the United States in establishing and maintaining efficient school systems, and otherwise promote the cause of education." It was sometimes characterized as an agency which gathered and published obsolete information which had little relevance to contemporary problems and was considered of little use to anyone except pedantic historians of education.

This point of view is not an entirely accurate perception of the historical functions of the Office. At various times it did have some responsibilities in relation to national goals and policies. It distributed some vocational funds, for example, and it encouraged programs in national emergencies, such as school programs in cooperation with the Federal Emergency Relief Administration during the depression and the Victory Corps during World War II. It devoted much of its energy to the study of educational problems, and some of its publications were landmarks in establishing directions both for administration and program development in the American schools. Its studies of state school finance did much to lay the foundation for improved programs in the state support of public education. Its studies of schoolhousing needs were used extensively on all levels of government, including the national. It initiated studies of the effects of existing school district organization and stimulated programs for the reorganization of school districts throughout the country. It established a common professional language for the description of educational, administrative, and school business procedures. Its studies of program needs of the schools were used extensively in curriculum evaluation and development, but there were those who thought that USOE had become too "progressive" in its orientation. Commercial enterprises which supplied the schools in various ways kept close lookout for its statistical reports and its forecasts of educational trends.

It was, however, a relatively small office with a modest budget and a limited staff. Most members were specialists in various areas of school operations. Except for some specialized grants, it had few regulatory functions, and it was always exceedingly cautious in exercising them. It provided specialized services, and it served in a resource capacity for any agency that needed information about the schools. Other factors to the contrary notwithstanding, those who knew how to use the resources of the Office respected it for what it did and the role that it performed. It was rarely a controversial factor in education or government.

The Office was called upon to advise on legislative matters affecting education on the national level and influenced educational legislation through reports it made to Congress. This was not a burdensome responsibility, since in the chronology of federal aid to education programs, the significant Congressional legislation was widely spaced for many years. In the nineteenth century, for instance, the First Morrill Act in 1862, the Second Morrill Act in 1890, and the establishment of the Army Medical School in 1893 were the only notable acts of educational consequence. Between 1900 and 1920, only seven acts were passed, the Smith-Hughes Act in 1917 being the most relevant to education in general. Between 1920 and 1940, there were eight acts, among which the most significant ones were the creation of the National Youth Administration, which gave part-time employment aid to youth, and the Civilian Conservation Corps, which provided vocational education in camps for out-of-school and out-of-work youth. By the 1940's the spacing was narrower, and there were 12 acts in the decade.

In 1946 alone, six acts of comparative moment were passed, all of them in the interests of scholarship and cultural exchange (e.g., the Fullbright Act and UNESCO Resolution). In the 1950's eight laws were passed, two of them providing for educational research: the creation of the National Science Foundation, which encourages and promotes basic research in sciences and education in the sciences (1950), and the Cooperative Research Act (1954), which established programs in the Office of Education for research, survey, and demonstration in the field of education. The passing of the National Defense Education Act, since amended and extended, was accomplished in 1958.

Then the escalation began. Between 1960 and 1965, thirteen important acts, six of them in 1964-65 alone, were added to the roster of educational legislation. Most relevant to the concerns of public school superintendents are the Civil Rights Act and the Economic Opportunity Act, both 1964, and the Elementary and Secondary Education Act, 1965.

Restructuring USOE

A study of educational legislation and its implications for the role of USOE reveals that (1) most of the funds allocated before 1964 were distributed on a formulary basis, and (2) most of the relationships which necessitated regulatory and discretionary authority by USOE before 1964 pertained to higher education. The role of the Office started to change dramatically when Congress began to appropriate money in much larger amounts for education and when some of these funds were allocated to specific institutions. Each institution, however, had to demonstrate to the satisfaction of the Office that it would use the money in accordance with the purposes established by Congress and in a manner superior to proposals made by other scholars or institutions.

The distribution of funds for federally impacted school districts did not constitute a change in normal procedures either under the Lanham Act of 1941 or the more recent versions of 1950. The old division of educational organization and administration was already set up to study administrative problems, and it could handle the new chores with little added assistance. As in other cases, the formula for distribution was incorporated into the law. The USOE merely had to interpret the law, devise forms and procedures for making application, check the applications for legal requirements and definitions of entitlement, and transmit authorizations. Decision-making called for the exercise of little discretion on the part of the staff. The USOE was accustomed to working this way.

This was not the case after the advent of research funds. Someone in the Office had to make decisions as to the best utilization of the funds for the achievement of the purposes of the Cooperative Research Act of 1954. A new agency whose functions were not within the scope of prior experience had to be established, and a new role for USOE had to be defined and implemented. The demand for the funds soon exceeded the authorizations. Under what circumstances could USOE accept certain proposals and reject others which had equally legitimate purposes? How does USOE play this discretionary role in a professionally competent and responsible fashion, when the local citizen knows that the federal government is a political enterprise and that his Congressional representatives are interested in representing their constituents' claims for federal sources of revenue before federal bureaus? It is extremely difficult to convince anyone who has a legitimate claim to federal funds that his proposals have relatively less merit than someone else's!

The issue of federal control has always served as a deterrent to the development of federal programs in support of education. When a federal agency develops criteria for the allocation of funds other than on a formulary basis, when it develops guidelines for the making of proposals and the distribution of authorizations, and when it exercises discretion on the basis of value judgments, it is certainly engaging in acts of control. One may find diplomatic language for its description, but in the final analysis it is saying to the relevant publics, "If you want to share in the funds, these are the conditions that you have to meet!"

Of necessity, USOE developed criteria for the selection of proposals and procedures for their screening, acceptance, and rejection. It was committed to the wise utilization of the research funds allocated to it for distribution and sought the improvement of education through the use of the limited funds available. Those who worked under the programs in the field sometimes chafed, sometimes criticized, but, on the whole, accepted the role of USOE, and many scholars were called upon to consult with the Office to help it maintain reasonable programs and desirable directions. As a federal agency, it was accountable to both the President and the Congress for how it distributed its funds and administered its responsibilities. Evidently, both Congress and the executive branch felt the programs were successful because successively larger amounts of money were authorized. Evidently, researchers and administrators in the field were also pleased with the program, because they mounted successive campaigns to support the program when continuation and extension were under Congressional consideration.

A new role had clearly evolved for USOE. In the first place, it developed some experience with "grantsmanship." The Office had become a funding agency, making its authorizations on discretionary rather than arbitrary formulary determinations. Secondly, the Office had, in effect, accepted (or been forced into) a new regulatory function, for it now had the responsibility not only to grant the funds, but to supervise the expenditure of the money and determine whether the contractual obligations of research agencies with the federal government had been fulfilled. Considering the limitations of the act and the characteristics of the program which had been established, few conflicts with institutions in the field actually arose. But the Office would never be the same again.

As mentioned before, most of the earlier relationships which necessitated regulatory and discretionary authority by the Office pertained to higher education. With the advent of the educational provisions of the Civil Rights Act of 1964 and the Elementary and Secondary Education Act of 1965, the Office began a new role in support of the work of the nation's schools. For the first time in its history, the Office had the responsibility for distributing large sums of money to state departments of education and directly to local school districts. Furthermore, while it had in the past provided various types of specialized aid to public instruction, particularly for vocational education, these were, by comparison, extremely modest interventions to stimulate desirable educational programs. Although USOE had been involved in approximately 16 major programs prior to 1965, the new programs established under ESEA with a massive infusion of money were many times larger than the sum of all the others.

In addition, although ESEA stated how much money could be allocated in each state, it ruled out any applications made on a purely formulary basis. The new law was highly specific. It violated the long standing principle of the educational profession, which opposed categorical aid by the federal government. General aid, on the other hand, was regarded as a different matter because funds could be distributed on the basis of a formula, hence minimizing federal discretion and the necessity for justification on the part of the local school district. In ESEA legislation Congress rejected general aid in preference to categorical assistance to the schools. Basically, the categories were to be as follows: (1) to improve programs for the culturally handicapped (as a part of the war on poverty), (2) to improve instructional materials and library services, (3) to stimulate the introduction of innovations and exemplary programs, (4) to expand the research capability of schools, state departments of education, and universities, and (5) to strengthen state departments of education.

Finally, ESEA was far more comprehensive in scope than any previous legislation. For example, the funds were made available to both public and private schools.

Congress had also passed the Civil Rights Act, and under Title VI of that Act, the Office was delegated the responsibility for the enforcement of the desegregation provisions in the public schools. The Act provided, in effect, that USOE was to establish guidelines for the total desegregation of schools, and failure of a school district to comply would result in the loss of all federal subventions. The Office thus became a dispenser of funds and a regulatory agency dealing with one of the most sensitive social issues confronting the country.

The Office had neither the staff nor the organizational structure necessary to meet all these new responsibilities. In the early days following the passage of ESEA, the Office was almost a counterpart of a western Gold Rush community. The demands upon staff were almost indescribable. From a relatively inconspicuous governmental bureau, it was forced into the limelight of public scrutiny. The task of dealing with Congress, alone, was monumental, not to mention the handling of numerous managerial details and public relations with new clientele, who descended upon Washington with empty but open money sacks.

The reorganization of the Office was inevitable, and when reorganization came, it was almost as though a bombshell had been exploded on Maryland Avenue. As far as staff was concerned, it was sudden, it was inexplicable, and it was drastic. It placed the Office in a state of confusion and appeared to have some ill effects upon the esprit of many employees. The effects of the reorganization have been documented elsewhere,[1] and they have only slight relevance to the problems explored here. The essential point is that the formal relationships within the Office were scrambled and at a time when massive responsibilities required immediate attention. The informal organization became confused. Since all employees are a part of the Civil Service, personnel were retained, but their responsibilities were changed. Directives were being formulated, but most

---

[1] See Stephen K. Bailey, *The Office of Education and the Education Act of 1965.* Inter-University Case Program #100. ((Indianapolis: The Bobbs-Merrill Company, 1966).

professional personnel on the Branch level did not receive direct communication from their superiors concerning the implications of the changes for their responsibilities. One informant, over a year later, stated that he did not agree with the shift; no one as far as he knew had outlined his new responsibilities; and his decision was to wait it out until the next reorganization came along. Fortunately, this attitude appears to exist among only a very small minority of the Office.

USOE organization—bureaus and office

As far as the people in the public schools were concerned, they would now be dealing with four distinct bureaus and one office. The bureaus were: (1) the Bureau of Elementary and Secondary Education, (2) the Bureau of Adult and Vocational Education, (3) the Bureau of Higher Education, and (4) the Bureau of Research. The office was the Office of Equal Educational Opportunities. The National Center for Educational Statistics was later established to develop newer means for carrying out the research, statistical, and data-gathering functions of the Office.

The Bureau of Elementary and Secondary Education was made responsible for the administration of Titles I, II, III and V of ESEA. In addition, it operated the Division of School Assistance in Federally Affected Areas and the Division of Educational Personnel Training, which was assigned the administration of National Defense Education Act training programs and the fellowship program for experienced teachers. More recently, the Bureau has also been assigned the development of the National Teacher Corps. For nearly all the newer programs, then, school administrators would be dealing almost exclusively with the Bureau of Elementary and Secondary Education.

The Office of Equal Educational Opportunities was involved directly with school districts in its regulatory functions related to segregation in the public schools. For vocational programs, school administrators dealt with the Bureau of Adult and Vocational Education, but operating patterns in this area had been developed over a period of time, and routines appeared to be well established.

Operational procedures—principles and policies

Obviously, USOE cannot deal directly with the some 25,000 school districts in the United States. The bureaucratic structure necessary to sustain such relationships would be unfathomable. Funds for Titles I and II of ESEA are allocated through state departments of education. Title III funds require approval of the state department of education and a direct involvement with the school district or compacts of school districts. The remaining programs, particularly under Title IV of ESEA, are related to school districts or their personnel only through state departments of education or colleges and universities.

To administer these programs, the Office developed certain operating procedures. In general, these procedures included the formulation of guidelines for submission of proposals, application or proposal forms and requirements, review procedures, and systems for determining the acceptance or rejection of proposals following review. Contractual and auditing procedures were developed in accordance with governmental regulations by the Contracts Branch, which operates as a managerial arm of the Commissioner's Office.

Several problems occurred in the definition of the roles of the Office. Obviously, it had to operate in such a manner that the funds would be made available to the agencies which could implement programs of ESEA. Operating procedures had to define among other details what services would be provided by the Office, what programs would be supported, and what reports and evaluations would be required. During the initial stages of implementing ESEA, superintendents were concerned whether the USOE would passively await the influx of proposals, once guidelines had been issued, or actively indicate specific areas of thrust, establish priorities, and actually solicit proposals in areas deemed most significant and from school districts with the highest potential for making significant breakthroughs.

ESEA specifically prohibits federal control over education. Consequently, in the development of its operating procedures and the determination of its roles, the Office had to be conscious of whether or not it could be charged with control rather than regarded as an agency acting in an advisory, consultative capacity.

Operational procedures—organizational hierarchy

For organizational purposes, USOE is hierarchically ordered. Each Bureau is headed by an Associate Commissioner who reports directly to the Commissioner. Within each Bureau are a number of Divisions, headed by a Division Director. Each Division, in turn, is divided into specific Branches, which are headed by Branch Chiefs. Some Branches are divided into Sections, headed by Section Chiefs. Presumably, the operating line of the Office is the Branch and its various sections. Supervisory and managerial roles are performed on the level of the Division, and policy-formation is, according to the formal organization, on the level of the Bureau.

Obviously, this is a complex organization. Technically, only the Commissioner speaks and is held accountable for the Office by Congress and the administration. He is directly responsible to the Secretary of Health, Education, and Welfare, and advises the Secretary and the President on educational legislation and problems. He is also called before Congress for evaluations of existing legislation, on departmental budgetary requests, on authorizations for continuing legislative programs, and on the appraisal of new legislative proposals. If Congress raises questions about internal operations, as it has about the enforcement of provisions of the Civil Rights Act, the Commissioner is the man who has to justify and defend the practices of his subordinates.

As far as the Office is concerned, the Commissioner operates on what Parsons terms the institutional level of the organization. He is several levels away from the Branches and Sections where contacts with the field take place. This is the level which links the organization with the broader social systems of which it is a part. It is obvious that his major focus is not upon the operating organization. He is its representative before many other groups. He is an arm of the executive branch of government. He influences internal policy. He can affect structural and organizational changes, and he can remove or re-assign personnel. But he cannot govern the day by day activities of all employees and their relationships to clientele systems in the field.

At the other end of the hierarchy are the professional employees of the Office who work in the Branches and Sections and perform the actual tasks for which the Office is established. To the publics with whom the Office has to deal, they are the "face" of the organization. Relatively few administrators are called upon to consult with the Commissioner. Many more will have some sort of direct contact with coordinators, consultants, and supervisors.

Between these two levels are the various policy-making, program maintaining, supervisory and coordinating personnel who point the directions for the organization.

Operational procedures—decision-making

Because of the complexity of the organization, it is inevitable that individuals of the lowest echelon of the hierarchy exercise considerable decisional responsibility. With what appears to be a paucity of coordinating and supervisory techniques in many Divisions and Branches, the individual coordinators may function with a fair degree of independence, formulating policies and relationships as they perceive their directives.

Changes in policy and thrust may be made some time in advance of the diffusion of general information about such matters throughout the organization. Even though there are review boards, the favorable or unfavorable reactions to proposals on the part of these individual coordinators may determine the acceptance or rejection of a project.

These personnel do not operate within a vacuum. They are subject to some constraints, although these may sometimes be rather loosely and sometimes rather rigidly interpreted. Some flow charts of procedures obviously exist somewhere in the organization. When, on several occasions, a member of the research team asked to see them, he was told that they did not exist, that they were unknown, or that they were in the process of being changed and were not currently available. Procedural directives do exist, and there is relatively little flexibility permitted on technical points. Contractual and auditing procedures, requirements, and expectations are succinctly spelled out. Over many of these technical details, the Office, itself, has little jurisdiction, since they have been worked out by other branches of government which are responsible for overall direction of such relationships.

As far as program requirements are concerned, personnel also must operate within the specifications of the guidelines which are established. These have been developed over a period of time and represent the combined efforts of a large number of people who are involved in a specific program. Before they are accepted, they are generally reviewed by panels of specialists selected from the educational field. Usually, well-qualified people are selected, and it was reported from all Divisions within the Office that very careful consideration is given to the recommendations of these panels. It is also apparent that specialists within the Office have been consulted, even though they may be outside of the Division or even the specific Bureau responsible for the development of the guidelines. Not infrequently individuals are "loaned" between Divisions or Bureaus to work on guidelines or the technicalities of specific programs.

The nature of the guidelines determines the course of the proposed project. Consequently, great care has been exercised in their formulation to avoid the charge of federal control of education. Personnel have paid close attention to the requirements of the acts and have studied proposed guidelines carefully in the light of their perceptions of the "intent of Congress" and the policies of the President.

It is difficult to pinpoint exactly where the final responsibility for guideline decisions rests. Ultimately, of course, they have to be accepted by the Associate Commissioner of the Bureau and by the Commissioner himself. On both levels, program planning and review staffs have carefully analyzed the guidelines and made recommendations. As is true with other critical issues, personnel below the level of the Associate Commissioners do not ordinarily wish to make a final decision. Those who can be identified with a particular decision are accountable for it before their peers, superiors, or even Congress. This can result in traumatic experiences. The defense against being held accountable is to involve, as extensively as possible, other personnel within the Office as well as experts from the field who are called upon for consultation and review. Recommendations arise from the Branch level, and staff work is done on this level. But the personnel in the Branches hasten to add that their work is passed on "up the line," and they do not know what happens to it when it leaves their hands. There is great reluctance among operating personnel to identify points of decision at least to "outsiders."

Guidelines are both facilitative and restrictive. They enable the Office to make decisions for the allocation of funds in accordance with general principles. They are restrictive in that they limit the kinds of projects that will be accepted as well as the range of discretion exercised by personnel within the Office on project acceptance. In effect, guidelines tell school administrators the conditions under which their districts may participate in federal programs.

This law, itself, imposes constraints upon USOE personnel inasmuch as it specifies purposes for which the funds are authorized, defines who may receive funds, and establishes under what general conditions recipients may use the moneys allocated to them. Since Congress generally makes annual authorizations of funds, each annual request for renewal of a grant must be accompanied with the record of accomplishments to date. Through hearings, studies, and investigations, Congress maintains vigilance over the Office and the utilization of the funds in the field. Therefore, personnel are compelled to make decisions that will receive favorable consideration from Congress and the President when the continuation of programs is at stake.

Within the requirements of the law, the limitations of personnel, and constraints of available budget, the Office has to decide how personnel will spend their time. Decisions have to be made relative to which roles can be performed, as well as which ones are most desirable.

The Office cannot be conducted as a private corporation or as a proprietary function of the personnel in charge. Care has been taken, both in the establishment of guidelines and the acceptance of proposals, to eliminate arbitrary or idiosyncratic decisions. This is accomplished through the employment of review panels, the selection of site evaluation committees from the field, the appointment of field readers who make recommendations, and the establishment of internal review and authorization committees to make recommendations for acceptance or rejection on the basis of their review of proposals and the recommendations received. Both Associate Commissioners and the Commissioner can review decisions, if they choose, and change the recommendations.

The elaborate structure of decision-making involves delays and a considerable amount of internal, managerial overhead. In special instances, where speed in decision-making is essential, a proposal can be "hurried" through. But this course is avoided, because personnel recognize that the overall procedure is a defense against the charge of favoritism or arbitrary decision. Complaints are frequently voiced about delays and red tape by administrators and researchers who wish to get started as soon as they have completed the proposal. These people may not recognize USOE for what it is—an understaffed governmental agency, charged with the responsibility for the just and equitable distribution of public funds, accountable both to Congress and the President, under scrutiny of the general public and its clientele, and faced with considerable pressures, both political and professional.

Field relationships

The great dilemmas faced by USOE arise from the issue of the relations which the Office shall have with those in the field. There are three schools of thought in the Office. One group maintains that the Office should restrict its activity to the barest requirements of a funding agency. It should receive projects, evaluate them, and if they are worthy, fund them. If they are not worthy, the Office should report to the appropriate state department of education the reasons for its action and state its recommendations for improvement. For the most part, this group feels that the Office should work exclusively, even in Title III projects, through state departments of education, since it cannot have effective field relationship with all of the school districts of the states. Neither can it communicate directly with all the districts which now or eventually will have projects funded by the government.

This position is fairly close to that taken by the Office on all funding projects under ESEA, with the exception of Title III. Under Title III there is a provision for field visits to assist school districts in the improvement of their projects. No districts among the sample of this study had had any direct field visits by Title III personnel. After negotiation of contracts, however, even under Title III, relationships with districts or with state departments of education decrease to almost zero, except for continuing pressures from the Office for evaluations of projects. It is held that visits to school districts are generally not feasible because of shortages of Office operating funds and personnel. Visits can generally be made only when the state department of education indicates severe malfunctioning of a project or misuse of funds. In this way, the Office stays out of the picture until the final reports or evaluations are submitted.

A second group holds that if USOE merely waits for proposals to come in, the purposes of ESEA will not be achieved. They believe that Congress intended that the funds be used to effect major changes in public education. They hold that the Office is charged with the responsibility for determining the areas of major thrust for which the funds will be used: One official stated:

> We are not passive recipients to the proposals that are sent to us. Ours is a role of leadership. Through our guidelines we are giving preference to such proposals as relate specifically to the educational and societal goals which we have accepted.

In this view, the guidelines are one but not the exclusive aspect of the leadership role of USOE. There is also some feeling that schools must be selected to participate in specific types of innovative programs and pilot experiments. In this view, the Office can perform three functions. First, it can solicit specific projects from specific agencies. Second, it can use whatever sources are at its command, including the judicious employment of grants and contracts, to encourage school districts to move in specific directions. Third, it can send out field representatives who will work with school districts, assisting them with the development of specific types of preferred projects. In this way, the Office will become a spearhead for determining directions of thrust, and it will use the power of the public treasury to achieve its ends.

A third point of view may be characterized as that of the "old-timers" in the organization, the personnel who date back to the period preceding the reorganization and the inundation occasioned by the passing of ESEA. These people hold that USOE cannot really be an effective funding agency when discretion has to be exercised. They believe that all federal funds should be allocated on a formulary basis so that discretion is removed from the Office. They feel that the Office exercises tremendous control over education through the use of the guidelines and that the guidelines cannot be realistically applied throughout the whole country. Some states are more advanced than others, and one set of guidelines, administered from Washington, inevitably results not only in more centralized dictation of educational policies, but also in exaggerating the differences that already exist among the states and school districts. Some have pointed out that present policies are already resulting in a regrettable situation wherein the more able school districts have the resources to develop proposals and negotiate them through either state departments of education or USOE, while the less fortunate school districts with limited financial and personnel resources are not the beneficiaries of federal aid to the same extent. However, in these smaller districts there is greater need of additional resources and, particularly, of enlarged staff for the improvement of instruction. The record to date indicates that there is a great deal of justification for this point of view, which maintains that the distribution of the money on a formulary basis would enable the states to make judicious financial distribution or even to use the money for the improvement of those school districts which have the greatest need. Whether or not USOE could, in accordance with the provisions of the Act, actually operate in this fashion is debatable.

This third point of view holds, in addition to its support of general rather than categorical aid that USOE should provide leadership for the improvement of education through the studies in which it engages and the publications which it distributes. They also point out that the resources of USOE should be used to make evaluations of the effects of federal legislation and to develop studies of educational conditions throughout the country. These reports could be used by Congress to consider further legislation and by various educational agencies to develop programs for the improvement of education in the country. It is felt that there is still a considerable need in the department for specialists who could make studies and work with state agencies in the improvement of programs and practices in the field. Those who held to this point of view had hoped that the National Center for Educational Statistics would fulfill this need. As of the time data were collected for this study, it had not as yet established its program to the degree which indicated that it would provide the detailed analyses of educational problems which were formerly available under the Division of Educational Organization and Administration.

It is quite evident that now, at least, the Office is operated under policies close to the first position but with tendencies toward the second. The guidelines clearly indicate some directions and preferred areas of concern, although they are not entirely restrictive. The massive structure of USOE is still not sufficiently large to exercise much supervisory service for school districts, although some is available in special areas. Field representatives to assist state departments are available under Title V. Field representatives are also available under Title III, but they cannot work with a large number of school districts and seem to spend most of their time holding conferences to explain the operations of ESEA to school administrators and consulting with new personnel in state departments of education who work with school districts in the development of projects and proposals. However, there is much concern in many quarters of the Office for a more explicit definition of the Office's leadership roles, for development of priorities in the improvement of education and the limiting of authorizations to priority areas, as well as a feeling of urgent need for expansion of staff, particularly in Title III operations, to enable the Office to have more direct relationships with school districts.

Several other basic problems confront USOE. The Office is currently set up to administer certain federal aid programs. As mentioned earlier, its massive effort must work out the operating procedures for getting the appropriated funds into the hands of school districts or other agencies which can develop the programs for which the money is allocated. Personnel and budgetary limitations, as well as continuing organizational problems, restrict the development of long-range programs for shifting educational needs. For these reasons, the educational specialists have been subordinated to the grant specialists. The educational specialists complain that the Office is now exclusively concerned with legislative programs and that it no longer forecasts, evaluates, and projects trends in the field, nor suggests desirable adjustments that need to be made. It is also averred that Congress or any other agency in the field could formerly request any information about education and find it readily available. The Office is still called upon to supply such information, but the grant programs have so handicapped the Office and so usurped its resources that the information is no longer available. Leadership and thrust in the Office have shifted from the areas of content to the areas of grants and contracts. In view of its new responsibilities, the Office can no longer afford the educational specialists. Many of them have left the Office, and those who remain have been reassigned. There is some feeling among those who remain—as well as among administrators and educational leaders in the field—that the Office is now less responsive to educational needs and that it develops its programs and policies with insufficient technical data about what is happening in education throughout the country.

The above analysis has not related to the operations of the Office of

Equal Educational Opportunities. Under Title VI of the Civil Rights Act, this Office has a much narrower assignment and provides basically a regulatory function. Its concern is limited almost exclusively to the enforcement of the desegregation provisions of the Act. In this capacity, it deals directly with school districts. It is charged with the responsibilities of developing guidelines, of obtaining evidence from school districts of compliance with the guidelines, and of recommending to the Commissioner the withholding of subventions from school districts which fail to comply. Limited funds are also available to the Office to support institutes for the training of personnel to deal with problems of integration and to develop model programs.

The extent of the problems of segregation in almost all sections of the country limits the amount of direct contact that the Office can have with individual school districts. Districts are asked to submit plans for compliance, to indicate readiness to comply, and to certify proposed progress is being made. Initially, the Office certified authorizations for disbursement of federal subventions on the basis of the school district's certification that it intended to comply with the provisions of the Act. Close scrutiny of compliance by each school district was an impossibility, and investigations were conducted in only those school districts where complaints were registered or where there was other evidence of failure of the district to operate in accordance with its certification. It is generally held by superintendents that this program is not working out well and that the Office cannot perform its responsibilities adequately with its present resources.

Relationships of USOE to Problems of Superintendents

In the complex structure of USOE there is a wide range of available resources which can be used to assist school administrators to develop strategies for dealing with their problems. There is a large number of competent people in the Office who have had broad experience in education, many of whom were specialists in educational administration previous to the reorganization of the Office. Some of them are recognized in the field as having made outstanding contributions to special areas of educational administration. Through its contacts with educational organizations and state departments of education, the Office has access to a great deal of information, and it could assess the degree to which various problems are barriers to the effective operation of the schools. Although some of its personnel are very much concerned, the Office itself seems not to be greatly involved.

Since the reorganization of the Office there is no single locus of concern about the problems of educational administration. There is no single agency within the Office which has the responsibility for the systematic identification of educational problems. There is no agency within the Office which systematically disseminates information about the efforts that are being made to solve problems uppermost in the minds of school superintendents or about the success various programs are having. There is a great deal of research financed by federal funds through the Office, but there is no agency which systematically disseminates the findings or makes them available in a form which can be used by professional educators or the public-at-large. There is no agency within the Office which allocates resources to the analysis of the implications of research for educational practices. Some of these functions may be fulfilled by either the National Center for Educational Statistics or the information network provided by the Educational Research Information Center (ERIC). Neither agency has been established long enough to determine what its actual impact upon the field will be, and whether it will relate sufficiently to administrators in the field or be more concerned with those programs beneficial to scholars of education.

It is recognized in the Office that many schools have deficiencies and that many problems exist which constitute barriers to effective operations or prevent the employment of the newer methods and the introduction of promising innovations. But the programs of federal aid to education are not administered in such a fashion as to take these problems into consideration or to provide means for their effective solution. One member of the staff pointedly observed, "We do not give much consideration to providing for the rectification of deficiencies just on the basis of need."

The concepts undergirding Title III programs apparently dominate the psychology of the Office. The key words in Title III emphasis are "innovation" and "exemplariness." Proposals are encouraged which will introduce innovations in the schools or which will develop exemplary programs from which, presumably, similar programs will generate. But no provision is made for the training of educational leadership. NDEA funds are used for institutes to improve the effectiveness of classroom teachers only. A few administrators are selected to participate in these institutes to improve their knowledge of specific content fields. But there are no institutes to improve the capabilities of administrators and to provide for improved leadership for managing change programs in the schools. In fact, this deficiency cannot be charged to USOE, since there is some question of whether or not institutes for administrators are beyond the limitations of the law.

It is difficult for the Office to maintain communications and direct relationships with the school districts of the country. The Commissioner attempts to maintain some contacts and periodically calls upon groups of administrators to consult with him. Relatively few can be invited, however, and they generally represent only the larger school systems of the country. Some administrators make trips to Washington to confer with program specialists about their problems in relation to federal programs. They generally receive the assistance which they seek. Findings indicate that the further the superintendents are geographically from Washington, the less contact they have, and the more difficult communication with the Office is.

The problems of the staff members of the Office are different from the problems of the administrators in the field. The staff member views the educational scene from a different perspective, and both staff members and administrators agree that it is frequently difficult for them to achieve congruence of their perspectives. Staffing the Office has become a problem of considerable magnitude, and priority has been given to the selection of people who can perform the functions of the Office rather than those who by virtue of their experience in the educational field are knowledgeable about the types of problems superintendents confront.

USOE does have field relationships with schools under regulatory programs pertaining primarily to the Civil Rights Act. There are also some modest field relationships under Title III, as previously indicated. Beyond these limited contacts, the Office is confined to working with school districts indirectly through state departments of education. It has direct relationships on a rather broad scale with state offices through various federal programs, such as Titles I, II, and V of ESEA. It provides some assistance both to state offices and to administrators in the field through such contacts.

Traditionally, USOE has worked directly with state departments of education. The establishment of regional USOE offices is an attempt to assign personnel who will specialize in the problems of the region they serve. But most state departments of education are notoriously weak and have an image of incompetence among the superintendents in the field and USOE staff members recognize this problem. Through Title V, funds are allocated for the improvement of state departments. However, given the politically-oriented leadership of many of the departments, the accumulation of weak personnel, and the failure of state legislatures to provide departments with the funds they need, the improvement of state departments of education will be a slow process unless some major revolution in their operating patterns takes place.

The link, then, between the Office and the field is weak, and the direct services are spotty and meager. Major thrusts of the Office are directed toward the introduction of innovations and developing model programs, but they are seemingly not related to the realistic everyday problems which claim so much of the time of the superintendents in the local school district. In fact, as previously indicated, superintendents reported that pressures from USOE to innovate have created serious problems for local school districts.

Superintendents' Perceptions
of USOE

Ten years ago, if one had asked the average administrator to describe USOE, he might have recited some facts he chanced to recall from his earliest textbooks on administration, or he might have pulled a pamphlet from the shelf which he had used. At that time the Office was remote to him; he had little direct or indirect dealing with it. He may have known the Commissioner's name, but no individuals within the Office stood out as distinct personalities. Today, superintendents are more aware of the Office, how it operates and what types of problems it causes them.

For the most part, the superintendents in our sample do not seem to be aware of the total bureaucratic structure of the Office. They perceive USOE as a large governmental entity, but they do not clearly differentiate its parts or how programs are managed among the various Bureaus, Divisions, and Branches. Since they do not separate it into parts, their references are almost always to USOE as a whole rather than to individual Divisions thereof. It has also been noted that for many of the superintendents the federal government's programs affecting the schools are all centered in USOE. Many do not clearly delineate between the Office of Economic Opportunity and USOE. Since OEO[2] has a much

---

[2] OEO is an independent branch of government which reports directly to the chief executive. The confusion on the part of superintendents is understandable since

poorer image among the school administrators than USOE, the latter is sometimes labeled with "guilt by association." Lacking an understanding in depth of how the Office of Education functions, they do not distinguish between policies of the Office and Congressional enactments. For example, they frequently blame USOE for timing problems which are, in fact, caused by Congress. Only a few superintendents in the sample studied have had direct, face-to-face contacts with personnel in the Office. They have made trips to Washington, or they have been involved in some conference where these contacts were made. It appears that these individuals feel less frustration in dealing with USOE than do the superintendents whose only contact may have been a conversation with a USOE consultant at a meeting called by the state department of education to explain federal programs. For the person who can get into Washington and establish contacts, the Office seems less formidable and remote.

On the whole, the superintendents apparently do not perceive the sources of authority within USOE. The Office itself is thought to make decisions. Occasionally vague references are made to the Commissioner but he appears to be too remote from their field of operations to fit into the picture. The source of authority to them is that person who makes decisions, and they want to deal directly with one person who can give them "answers." Since the consultant or coordinator with whom they correspond often cannot make the decision himself, superintendents sometimes feel as though they are getting the "run around," and "no one is in authority in the outfit." There is some feeling that the regional offices, as they are emerging, are a potential source of improvement because they will bring personnel and decisions closer to the schools throughout the country; but, to date, there appears to be some frustration in working with the regional offices, because personnel in them "can't give you the answers."

In addition to some misperceptions of the organizational structure of the office and its methods of operation, superintendents seem to have some very definite points of view regarding the personnel. It should be stated here that there are feelings of respect for the top leadership of the Office and impressions that personnel generally want to be helpful.

In only two ways was the leadership criticized. First, there is much

USOE and OEO have a *Memorandum of Agreement*, which specifies cooperative arrangements on various "War on Poverty" projects. Head Start and Upward Bound projects are particularly involved. The role of USOE appears to be advisory, however, since funding is under Title II-A of the Economic Opportunity Act of 1964. Responsibility for the operation of these programs is vested in OEO.

criticism of personnel who perform the regulatory functions of the Office of Equal Educational Opportunity. They are sometimes described as aggressive, overbearing, and accusatory. Whether there is justification for this perception, or whether it comes from educators who have been forced to comply with Civil Rights Act provisions, is a matter of conjecture. It is suspected that the attitude arises out of a contentious situation, and that USOE representatives toward whom the superintendents charges are directed might make similar charges.

A second criticism stems from a concern of administrators and professors of educational administration about the backgrounds of some key executives in the Office. A professional group tends to be a closed corporation and is resentful of individuals who have authority in their field but do not belong to the profession. Several executives of USOE have not been recruited from education. Superintendents have fears that their appointments were politically inspired, that they do not adequately understand the culture in which the schools operate, and that they are responsible for creating barriers to effective rapport between administrators in the field and USOE.

Superintendents seem to recognize that the Office has faced some tremendous problems of staffing. But they do expect that agencies which exercise authority over them will employ personnel whose professional competence they respect and in whose professional judgments they have confidence. They resent being told that their proposals are not acceptable by someone who lacks their own experience and does not indicate an understanding of the problems of the field. One superintendent summarized a number of his peers' perceptions when he said:

> They need people who understand the problems of running schools and can talk with us in our language. Sometimes they lack understanding of local problems and conditions. . . . They frequently send out people to work with us who aren't qualified to get a job in our school district.

Superintendents also complained about the apparent shortness of tenure of Office personnel with whom they have had direct communication. One superintendent expressed a concern, also frequently mentioned by others, when he said: "The U. S. Office has always been an enigma to me. The guys who are directing activities are only temporarily stopping there. It's a sort of Grand Central Station."

There is only slight variation in perceptions of the services rendered by USOE. Other than its modest communications with respect to grants, the Office is not highly visible in the field. Several superintendents said that they had no contacts with USOE except to ask for money. Some indicated that the Office is not a force for working with the public schools except through specific grant programs. Some still remember it for its publications and its statistical services. Some indicated that if you wished to cut through the red tape and go directly to Washington, you could obtain some valuable assistance from personnel. Some indicated that since the Office is politically oriented rather than professionally inspired, it does not place much emphasis upon its relationships to the field or provision of those services most needed in the field.

A number of superintendents recognize that the Office cannot possibly work with all of the school districts in the country. However, superintendents from the larger school districts, where the greatest discontent with state departments of education seems to prevail, resent that they cannot always work directly with the Office. They see evidence of USOE working increasingly through state departments, but they do not feel that school districts will be adequately served through the state departments. They feel that they would obtain services more suitable to their needs if they could work directly with personnel in USOE. This is one hope that they have for the regional offices of USOE. If the regional offices are given sufficient authority and staffed with people who understand the problems of administrators in the field, the administrators are confident that they can make effective use of their services.

Many superintendents recognize that although they have had many managerial problems that arise from federal programs, these programs have been exceedingly beneficial in the improvement of local schools. NDEA institutes and programs for upgrading instructional materials and services were cited frequently. The statement was made that "The USOE has demonstrated that it can conduct programs which are good for education, but it is not adapted to conducting hand-holding operations." Some think that it is a good thing that it is not so adapted, because the provision of extensive consultative and other field services by USOE personnel would mean the enlargement of the bureaucracy, either in Washington or in regional offices, whose services would duplicate or be in conflict with those of state departments of education. The smaller schools—those below the level of the larger metropolitan centers—especially prefer to see the state departments become the intermediaries for USOE. They feel that the state departments are likely to be more responsive to their needs and to their points of view. They also recognize that USOE cannot have the same type and consistency of services with all school districts in the country. Particularly as a result of the policies for the enforcement of the Civil Rights Act, it is recognized that re-

lationships would have to be uneven and that ill-will would be engendered.
Some superintendents recognize the effort that had to be made within
the Office to enable it to operate its programs as effectively as it does.
One superintendent said:

> The Office of Education is more effective than we gave it credit for be-
> ing in the conference. We are critical of the guidelines on desegregation,
> but it has done a lot of good through ESEA. We could write a better law,
> but with all its imperfections, the Office has made great strides. It was
> never before in a leadership role—not even with state departments of edu-
> cation—and it has had to make some tremendous adjustments and de-
> velop into new areas of concern. It was extremely difficult to open up so
> many new programs and employ as competent a staff as they have.

Criticisms of the Office as a whole were expressed in two specific
areas. First, it was felt that school administrators were definitely barred
from in-service education activities sponsored by USOE. Teachers have
opportunities to participate in the NDEA institutes and training programs sponsored by the Office through state departments of education.
Superintendents felt that USOE has exerted leadership to obtain these
institutes and other specialized training programs for teachers, but has
done nothing to provide funds for the in-service education of administrators. As a result, some superintendents felt that their principals were not
keeping pace with their teachers.

Second, they expressed concern for the educational research sponsored
by USOE and its practical application in the schools. Many expressed
the feeling that great sums of money have gone into basic research, and
research and development centers, but that no one has taken the responsibility for the dissemination of the findings to the school districts. The
statement was made that the personnel from USOE do much talking about
the lag between knowledge and practice in education, but they haven't
mounted any programs to help administrators identify the practices which
need to be changed or the new knowledge that needs to be applied.
Although they are not asking for less basic research, they want more
emphasis on applied research and development.

There is a noticeable difference between the opinions of state superintendents of public instruction and local school district superintendents.
Most state superintendents perceive USOE as an agency which works
directly with state departments of education providing them additional
resources for program improvement. They see the Office as using its
resources effectively, for the most part, when it engages the state departments of education as intermediaries to work with the public schools.

Some of the state superintendents are critical of Title III policies, under which the Office works directly with school districts, although approval of the projects by state departments is mandatory by law. Title III is the only ESEA program that does not stipulate that the proposals from local districts be in accordance with a state plan.

Local superintendents are divided on most of these issues. As previously indicated, the superintendents of the larger school districts prefer to have independent relations with the Office rather than to work through the state departments. Since many of the larger districts have the resources to send representatives to Washington and establish visible, direct relationships with USOE, superintendents from smaller school districts complain that the Office favors the larger school districts. They also argue that the guidelines and procedures for developing proposals handicap the smaller but aid the larger school districts. The smaller school districts are notoriously understaffed for administration, and they do not have the resources they need for proposal development. Neither do they have the resources nor the number of federal grants to justify employing full-time administrators to deal with federal programs. They complain that the failure of the guidelines to incorporate administrative costs or to allow overhead makes it extremely difficult for them to take full advantage of federal programs. They argue that these factors result in an uneven distribution of federal aid, the lion's share going to those school districts that are most capable of mounting programs even without the federal subventions.

The strengthening of state departments is more generally recommended by superintendents than is the extension of the regional offices to the point where they displace the state departments. Much hope is expressed for the roles that can be played by the regional educational laboratories, but there is some fear that they, like the R and D centers, are more inclined toward basic research than toward the real needs of the field. There is also some fear that USOE is creating instrumentalities, such as regional offices and regional educational laboratories, whose policies may be in conflict with those of the state departments. They realize that whereas USOE will be able to exercise considerable authority over laboratories and offices, state departments of education must remain responsive to local concerns.

There is some evidence that superintendents fear the strengthening of any agencies which are beyond their control. They cling to the concept of local control of education, and they resist the strengthening of legal entities of the state or federal governments that have the potential for limiting that control. If any agencies are to be strengthened, they would prefer that they be those over which they can have the most influence.

Many concerns about USOE stem, it seems, from traditional fears of federal aid to education. Most administrators seem to recognize that the federal programs in which they are engaged are desirable and have helped the schools channel programs into areas which are of critical importance, but into which they would not have ventured because of their limited school district funds. Nevertheless, administrators are concerned about being able to deal directly with the Office because of its present and potential regulatory functions. They see the guidelines as having imposed too many restrictions and directives upon them. They feel that these federal programs have resulted in some imbalances in their own instructional programs, and that they have robbed basic educational programs of a portion of the resources which should have been allocated to them.

Summary

Since 1965, USOE has become a substantial force in education, and superintendents as well as state departments of education have to learn to work with it. As the administrative agency which distributes a vast amount of public money dedicated to the support of specific types of educational programs, USOE has assumed a major responsibility for directing the future course of education in the United States. Whether or not their policies are in accordance with the "intent of Congress," it was almost inevitable that the Office take this leadership, considering the few constraints imposed by the legislation.

USOE has become a major funding agency. The greatest responsibility of the Office now is one of determining the allocation of funds to the clientele who can legitimately and effectively use them. It is faced internally with the necessity of mobilizing its resources for coordinated action, and externally with the necessity of working within an ethos that harbors suspicions about the intentions, as well as integrity, or centralized control. Many USOE officials feel that in order to discharge their responsibilities for the wise allocation of federal funds, they must also exercise leadership in establishing the goals to be realized with the use of the funds. Superintendents, and probably the school boards which they represent, feel that their authority over educational policies on the local level is being eroded at an accelerating pace. They fear that the increasing power occasioned by the exercise of discretion in the distribution of federal funds will result in the federal government's establishing further regulatory functions with which local districts will have to conform. The Office is also caught in the dilemma of how best to utilize its resources as a funding agency. It will take an even more extensive bureaucracy than now exists or is visualized to provide the supervisory and resource assistance which local school districts may need. By either building such a bureaucracy or by strengthening regional offices, USOE may be able to reduce the feeling of remoteness and exert a greater impact.

Either method raises the danger of more intense charges of federal control. On the other hand, traditional methods of working with state departments of education are ineffective because of the weaknesses of those departments. There is little likelihood that the state departments will improve rapidly enough to become effective arms of USOE and reliable sources of leadership for the schools.

It must be recognized that there are several significant barriers to the effective operations of USOE for reaching superintendents and aiding them with their problems.

First, the Office is highly vulnerable politically. It is subject to close scrutiny by both legislative and executive branches of the federal government. When Congress decides to find a scapegoat or to put on a dramatic political show for the constituents back home, the results can effectively wreck the morale of an executive department. On Civil Rights legislation, for example, the Commissioner of Education has been a convenient whipping-boy. The executive branch, as well, can use the Office as an exculpatory device. Obviously, this political fencing produces insecurities within the Office, makes educational legislation a tool of irrelevant political forces, and promotes the concept of rule by expediency rather than by long-term, systematic planning with the agency.

The Office is also vulnerable by reason of the political activity of its clientele. Congressmen encourage their constituents to keep them informed of their relationships with federal agencies. Clientele have frequently interpreted this to mean that Congressmen will use their political power to intercede in their constituents' behalf. While the Office attempts to protect itself, it cannot always resist such political pressures. Unfortunately, there will be occasions when officials who suggest positive programs, adopt a frank and honest attitude toward the clientele, or exhibit an aggressive professional leadership in encouraging change will be censured for their actions.

Second, the Office cannot realistically engage in long-range planning. As indicated in Chapter II, one of the grimmest problems encountered in federal aid programs is the "hand-to-mouth" basis of support. Congress makes annual appropriations. The President presents an annual budget to Congress. When national emergencies arise, the executive or Congress must find less essential expenditures which can be diverted. Program administrators in the Office must, inevitably, live on a hope and a prayer, not because of the bureaucracy or their own ineptitude, but because the exigencies of being a part of the federal government and subject to its political relations allow it no other *modus operandi*.

Third, the Office is affected by instability of leadership. An agency subjected to political control has to have a leadership which is expendable. Certainly the Commissioner and the Associate Commissioners know they live in glass houses built on shifting sand and that they, themselves, are replaceable. Such changes have occurred and will undoubtedly reoccur. Everyone in the Office knows this, and there are even some speculations about "setting the dates."

The instability of leadership is related not only to the political forces impinging upon it, but to the forces operating within the bureaucracy. The Civil Service employees who study the bureaucracy very carefully, are aware of the fact that the top jobs in the organization appear to be closed to them. Occasionally, one may rise to the position of Division Director, but all recent associate commissioner appointees have been from outside the Office. The old Roman adage, *novus rex, nova lex*,[3] is certainly applicable. Changes in leadership result in changes of policy and thrust. The bureaucracy persists. The Civil Service, despite its weaknesses, provides stability and security of programming both for employees and clientele of the Office. Major shifts may not gain the support of the Civil Service. Since the reorganization, there is evidence that in some areas personnel have resisted acceptance of thrusts desired by the new leadership. This makes for frustrations among the clientele and less than full effectiveness internally. Executives say one thing for the press, but coordinators do not always act on the basis of such policies. It is important to note again, that the Civil Service employees tend to be the "face" of the organization. Tenure even among them has been less stable than customary since the reorganization. Clientele can readily pick up the feeling that all present relations with people and policies are temporal and that significant changes can be expected.

Fourth, the Office has not as yet worked out the problems of establishing adequate liaison and rapport with the field. As previously indicated, it cannot realistically establish direct relationships with every school district in the country. To attempt to do so would mean the estab-

---

[3] A new king, a new law.

lishment of field offices in every state and very serious difficulties with state departments of education and local political forces would ensue. The Regional Offices may supplement, but politically they dare not attempt to supplant, state departments of education. With all of their weaknesses and inadequacies, state departments of education will have to remain the linkages between USOE and the field. It is unlikely that state departments of education will receive the funds they need for their own improvement from any source other than the federal government. Their improvement, then, is a matter of prime urgency for the realization of the goals established by Congress and the President for the improvement of education. The accomplishment of this end will necessitate considerable strengthening of the Division of State Agency Cooperation within USOE and a modification of some of its operating procedures and perspectives. USOE must also sooner or later face the fact it has initiated programs in almost all areas except that of improving the administrative capabilities of those who are charged with exercise of leadership on the operating level of the public schools. USOE personnel (among all the other groups who make the superintendent fair game) have not been reluctant to criticize them for their failures to give adaptive leadership to their schools. Superintendents play key roles in the direction of educational change, but no funds have been allocated, nor as far as we can determine, requested, for in-service education of superintendents, for the provision of services which can help them systematically analyze and interpret their problems, for the implementation of research, or for their experimentation with various types of administrative strategies. A few examples can be cited of direct USOE relations with school districts or interest in administrative problems. But these are scattered and inconsistent. They relate only infrequently and indirectly to the superintendent and his problems.

If the question is asked, "What agency in USOE is basically concerned about the improvement of educational administration for the purpose of improving the nation's capability for educational leadership," the answer is, "We haven't been able to discover it!" The Office has become program-centered rather than issue-centered. It deals with the management of programs for funding purposes, and it does not appear to extend itself much beyond these programs. It is fumbling with the problems of its own leadership roles, but neglecting to give guidance for the improvement of leadership in school districts where its programs must be implemented.

Perhaps the difficulty lies in the fact that USOE has become too much dominated by the grantsmanship philosophy to avoid the pitfalls experienced by the private foundations, which gave money copiously to impose solutions to educational problems, but failed to give educational leadership the resources or time to develop their human capabilities and the technologies essential for effecting major changes in the educational enterprise.

4 /

State Departments of Education
and Their Services
to Superintendents

Traditional Role of State Departments of Education

From its earliest origins in this country, education has been recognized as a function of the state. In those colonies where public schools existed, the colonial governments imposed upon local communities certain educational obligations. The colonial legislatures prescribed both structures of governance and standards and conditions for the maintenance of public schools. But by the time of the adoption of the federal constitution in 1789, the pattern had been accepted in the Middle Atlantic and New England colonies that public schools would be governed under the regulations enacted by state legislatures and that local tax units would be established both to support and administer the schools as arms of the state.

As the public schools expanded, the legislatures established a state educational agency with limited powers and functions over public education within the state. Because of geographical size and distances, as well as difficulties of transportation and communication which existed prior to World War I, state educational agencies could not effectively operate all of the schools in the state. Only three basic functions seem generally to have been delegated to them.

First, they have been assigned certain *regulatory* functions. It is their responsibility, generally, to enforce state laws and to require reports from local school districts indicating the extent to which state laws have been enforced. One of their most important regulatory functions has been the administration of certification requirements for teachers. They have also been charged with the responsibility of developing and enforcing the use of state courses of study and state-adopted textbooks.

Secondly, the state departments have an *inspectorial-supervisory* function to perform. It has been their responsibility to inspect the public schools and to provide some supervisory services to assist local school districts when needs arise, to evaluate the instructional effectiveness of local schools, and to check upon the enforcement of state regulations.

Thirdly, the state departments of education have played *appellate* roles with respect to the decisions made by local school district boards and administrators. State laws generally provide that citizens and employees can appeal local decisions to the state superintendent or department of education. These have always been considered vital roles to insure a check on the possible arbitrary or abusive use of authority by local school officials.

These functions suggest that the traditional roles of the state department of education have been both to represent the interests of the state in the maintenance of public schools and to protect the teacher, citizen, or child against arbitrary, abusive, or indifferent performance of educational responsibilities by local officials.

However, a systematic theory of the functions of the state with respect to education was never clearly articulated. The culture of the local school district fostered the neglect and subordination of the state educational agency. Local school districts were developed to administer and operate the schools, and they began to guard their responsibilities jealously and to assume that they had legal right to the control of public education. State functions were allocated on a limited basis to insure that no locality would be forced to provide more than minimal levels of education for its children and that maximum flexibility could be exercised by the local school district. The regulatory functions of the state departments were looked upon as efforts of a centralized bureaucracy to restrict the freedom of local decision-making.

In the history of the development of the American school system, state superintendents of public instruction (or commissioners of education) and the state departments of education over which they preside have almost always been a subject of controversy. The state departments have assumed various roles, depending upon the perspectives and ability of the particular state superintendent, but only infrequently has the office emerged as a vital force for the improvement of education within the state. The fortunes of the state office have seemed to fluctuate with the strength and weakness of the incumbent superintendent. Periods of ascendancy, growth, and leadership have been followed by longer periods of decline, retreat, and ineptitude.

In their periods of dynamic leadership, state departments of education have forged important political roles for themselves by the recommendation of state legislation in support of public education and the development of their own resources to assist local schools in the solution of problems and the improvement of the quality of education. Among the accomplishments that can be credited in large measure to the leadership of some state departments are: (1) the improvement of certification requirements for teachers and the general upgrading of the quality of the teaching profession; (2) the reorganization and development of a system of more efficient school districts; (3) provision of consultative services in the content areas of the curriculum to assist school districts in the improvement of their educational programs; (4) the development of regulations to protect the health and safety of children; and (5) the provision of a variety of administrative services to assist rural school boards and superintendents in the development of adequate school building programs and administrative services.

Nevertheless, the record is fragmentary and inconsistent. For the most part, the role of the state departments of education has been more that of a "gate-keeper" of the *status quo* than one of dynamic leadership. Most frequently, state superintendents and their departments have been tools of the legislature to hold education in check and to prevent a strain on the state treasury. On the whole, neither much leadership nor pointing of directions for the improvement of education was expected of them.

Emerging Role of
State Departments

In recent years, there has been a tendency for the state department of education to perform a more forceful leadership role in the maintenance of public education. This leadership role is not often defined, but there has been a general trend for the states to establish specialized resources which can be used to formulate program improvements and advise local administrators, school boards, and teachers in the solution of their problems; to provide in-service educational programs needed to upgrade the quality of educational performance within the state; and to establish research and informational services to assist school districts and to aid state legislatures on educational legislation.

Since 1958, when the NDEA programs began, the state departments of education have assumed increasing responsibilities for the allocation of federal funds to school districts, for assisting school districts in the development and evaluation of proposals for federal programs, and supervision of contractual relationships between the federal government and local school districts.

These extended responsibilities have seemingly broadened the scope of the functions of the state departments of education. They have increasingly become intermediaries for the federal government in practically all of the federal programs in aid to elementary and secondary education. Personnel have been added, and the federal government, particularly under Title V of ESEA, has provided funds specifically to state departments of education for the improvement of their services.

Federal programs have had their effect upon all state departments of education from which data were gathered for this study, but not to the same degree. It is, again, apparent that programs vary depending upon the nature of the leadership of the departments. Some departments have readily accepted the new challenges imposed by ESEA as an opportunity to expand and improve their services. Others have followed more reluctantly. All have apparently wanted to take advantage of federal funds for the improvement of education within the states. For the most part, they appear to have responded very positively to their responsibilities in the war on poverty. Except for the more restrictive programs developed under OEO, funds provided by the federal government have been administered fairly independently by the states, although departments vary in their ability to handle the funds effectively.

On the other hand, relatively few departments have developed programs to support the federal government in a basically regulatory function. In the enforcement of the desegregation provisions of the Civil Rights Act, which provides funds only in support of its regulatory provisions, state departments of education have frequently been one of the most serious deterrents to the accomplishment of the purposes of the legislation. In these cases the federal government has had to assume practically all of the responsibilities. Failure of most states to respond has practically forced USOE to deal directly with school districts on matters of desegregation.

In this area of desegregation there is evidence of an emerging role which the state departments could perform in expanding their leadership functions. For various reasons—which we assume are mainly political—with few exceptions, they have failed to do so. This fact raises the question of the future roles of state departments of education: Will state departments of education be able to give vigorous leadership to finding solutions to the critical and controversial issues confronting school administration? Or will they continue to confine their operations to the traditionally safe and respectable areas? A review of local superintendents' perceptions of state departments of education may give some clues to the future.

School Superintendents' Perceptions of the
State Department

For the most part superintendents in our sample perceive state departments of education as primarily regulatory, rurally-oriented, politically-dominated, unreliable, and ineffective. They see attempts made by the state departments of education to offer a range of services, but because of the inadequacies of both numbers and quality of personnel, these services are generally very lightly valued. With one exception, none of the superintendents could identify ways in which the state departments of education systematically study the problems of school administrators and attempt to develop consistent programs for assisting administrators in the solution of their problems. Perceptions of the manner in which the state departments conduct their regulatory functions varied. In some states, the state departments are considered arbitrary and restrictive in the enforcement of regulations, while only in a very few states are they credited with being flexible and understanding.

In practically all the states, the department employs a staff of consultants to assist school districts in the development of educational programs in the various content fields of the curriculum. Some states have consultants in specific areas of specialization in school administration, such as school law, school plant planning and business management. Superintendents evaluations of these services differ widely. In some states, these services are looked upon as very helpful and competent, while in others they are considered to be less effective than the specialized resources available in the school districts themselves.

Practically all states provide some types of workshops or in-service education programs for administrators. In very few instances, well-devised programs which include cooperation with major universities in the state have been developed. Generally, however, these programs are designed primarily to communicate to superintendents information about legislative programs or the enforcement of regulatory provisions. Some endeavors are made to provide workshops for new administrators chiefly to orient them toward the legal requirements of their jobs. Some states are developing centralized data processing services which are viewed as both desirable and helpful. In many states, emerging research departments are regarded with mixed feelings by superintendents because of their apparent preoccupation with "social bookkeeping."

In all but three of the 22 state departments of education studied, the leadership of the state department of education is judged to be inadequate. The state departments of education are generally labeled as weak, especially in the areas of planning, development, and research.

The appellate roles of the state departments of education are also viewed in different lights. Superintendents would like to have the state departments of education serve as buffers between the school districts and the various publics with which the school district is concerned. In some states, the state departments of education, and particularly state superintendents of public instruction, are said to be supportive of the schools and helpful in maintaining satisfactory public relations. In other states, it is felt that the state departments of education are highly politically oriented and inclined to sacrifice the reputation of the public schools in order to safeguard their own favorable political images. Protest groups frequently contact the state departments of education, and superintendents fear that weak and politically conscious officials give them assistance in their efforts to embarrass local administrators and school boards.

It is generally acknowledged by superintendents that services of state departments of education have greatly expanded as a result of augmented programs of federal support. Superintendents recognize that additional personnel in state departments of education are providing increasingly desirable services to help school districts prepare adequate proposals for federal projects.

To most local superintendents in the sample, the problems of the state departments of education arise from three primary sources. First, the state departments of education are looked upon as being too deeply involved in politics, particularly in those states where the state superintendent of public instruction is elected by the people or appointed by a political official. There is some feeling that political concerns restrict the effective leadership of state superintendents. In one state, it was indicated that the state superintendent of public instruction was appointed by the governor and replaced every four years. This produced instability in the orientation and program of the state department of education and eliminated the potential for effective planning. It is also felt that the political concerns of department personnel interfere with their assuming adequate professional roles and responsibilities.

Where the state superintendents are concerned about their political relations, there is a feeling that the state departments of education avoid effective involvement in important issues and side-step strong leadership either in the development of adequate legislative programs or the formulation of major approaches to the solution of educational problems, or both. One group of superintendents charged that because the state superintendent is elected, the entire apparatus of the state department of education is involved in his re-election for a period of six months prior to the election while the provision of services to the school districts ceases.

Secondly, superintendents feel that legislative support for state departments of education is grossly inadequate. Salaries are low, and the ability to provide the range of essential services is restricted. The superintendents feel that state departments of education occupy a relatively low status among governmental services and that, because of this, they rate a low priority in the allocation of scarce financial resources. It is recognized by some superintendents that the inadequacy of financial support has, in some instances, been intentional rather than merely negligent, that rurally-dominated legislatures have deliberately restricted funds to state departments of education to keep them weak and ineffective. In this way, it is contended, the legislatures have insured that the departments can provide only minimal leadership of or control over local school districts.

The third factor, and possibly the most significant one in the superintendents evaluation of the state departments of education, relates to the adequacy of personnel. The superintendents feel that because salaries are inadequate, state departments of education cannot obtain the services of the best qualified people within the state. Low salaries also result in very high turnover of personnel. As professional employees achieve greater experience, education, and competence, they tend to move to better paying positions. Many superintendents maintain that the most competent personnel are thus constantly drained off, leaving the least competent as the career employees of the department.

There is also a feeling that the personnel do not inspire confidence because they come from small school districts and have inadequate administrative or educational experience. Some superintendents charge that older administrators who have been ineffective in their positions, retreat to the state department of education when "things get tough." They maintain that the top educators in the state do not consider an appointment to the state department of education as an advancement. It is also felt that employment in the state department of education is sometimes for patronage rather than for sound professional leadership qualities. Persons receive appointments because of political services rendered to state superintendents rather than because they are the best qualified for the position. In many instances, they are not competent to perform the responsibilities for which they were employed. Several states have programs for supervisory evaluations of schools, and administrators were highly critical of being evaluated by state supervisors who had had no basic preparation for this service and whom they considered less competent than local principals and supervisors.

In a few states, superintendents recognize that salary schedules are competitive and personnel are eager and able to help local school districts with their problems. In these states, however, the demands for such services exceed the supply of people available to render them. One state department provides highly competent survey services for local school districts but the demand for these services is so great that the department is running from three to five years behind schedule.

In spite of many of the criticisms of the state departments by superintendents, relationships between them appear to be fairly cordial. In those few states where the superintendents place high value on the services of the state departments of education, it was stated that very close and effective interaction takes place. In states where superintendents have to deal with regulatory agencies other than state departments of education (such as mediation boards in Michigan and Wisconsin), they stated that they would prefer to deal exclusively with state departments on all educational and regulatory concerns. In the other states, it was obvious that relations depend upon the quality of the personnel and the nature of the services that are provided. For instance, it was pointed out that in New York the Commissioner, himself, maintains constant contact with the administrators in the school districts and that he has a large staff of resource people who work closely and effectively with the school administrators, assisting them with their problems and developing programs that enable them to improve their operations. Superintendents in this state also indicated that the state department of education plays a vital role in helping local school districts maintain effective rapport with their various publics. Furthermore, the state department in New York has been responsive to the needs for additional financial resources and has worked effectively with both the governor and the legislature to attain them. Effective assistance is rendered in regard to federal aid programs, and the Commissioner has established services to assist districts in complying with federal regulations. There is some feeling among school superintendents in the state that not all personnel are adequate for their responsibilities, and that more personnel are needed. On the whole, however, superintendents value the assistance rendered and would like to have more.

In contrast to the situation in New York State, are the reports from superintendents in another state, who maintain that the state department provides no effective leadership and is political in its orientation. Local superintendents in this state contend that the state department of education has inadequate personnel, most of whom are older, former superintendents who were not able to take the pressure of the superintendency and have retreated to the state department of education prior to their retirement. Resources for working effectively with the school districts in this state are meager, and school districts generally lack confidence in the advice offered by personnel from the state department of education. Superintendents feel that this state department of education staff is so weak that it cannot give effective assistance to the school districts in securing federal programs. One superintendent said that this state department of education erects road blocks to prevent the school districts from obtaining federal assistance.

The larger school districts generally reported that they do not use the resources of the state departments of education because their own resources are superior to those of the state department. In many instances, they had examined the credentials of personnel from the state department of education and found them lacking in the qualifications which are desired for similar positions in their own districts. It was pointed out by a number of the superintendents of the larger school districts that they have loaned resources to the state departments of education in order to assist them with their problems and programs. Some said they give assistance to state departments rather than receive it.

State departments of education were also criticized by the superintendents in the larger districts for being rurally-oriented. The personnel have had, for the most part, no experience in working with the larger school districts. Their sympathies and perspectives are aligned with the rural areas, and they widen the chasm between the larger school districts and the rural areas, particularly in the realm of school finance. These superintendents point out that leadership in educational affairs, even in legislative concerns, comes from the superintendents of larger school districts, not from state departments of education. Without assistance of personnel from larger districts, developmental programs of state departments would often fail. At least one state department official recognized a real dilemma in this matter. He asserted that larger districts do not want the services of the department, and that rural areas are so weak in leadership that communication with them is almost impossible.

It was further pointed out that most state departments of education offer no basic assistance on critical problems and leave the administrators pretty much to their own devices. This was especially true on such issues as integration and teacher militancy. Smaller school districts are particularly in need of strengthened state departments and have benefited from whatever improvements have been made. For instance, these districts lack the resources for developing programs for the utilization of federal funds and many have found the services of state department personnel to be particularly beneficial.

In summary, the superintendents who were interviewed for this study generally feel that the state departments of education could render better service than they are now giving and that it is imperative that the leadership of the state departments of education be improved. They believe that federal funds have been of value in the strengthening of the state departments of education, but contend that not enough has been accomplished. They would like to see the state departments of education improve their consultative services, both in the content areas of the curriculum and also in the direct provision of assistance to administrators. They feel that the efforts of state departments of education to provide centralized data processing and information services have been successful and that these services will be of increasing value to school districts. They also contend that state departments of education should be able to provide additional research services, in which particular emphasis is placed upon personnel. They are hopeful that state departments, with the cooperation of universities, will be able to provide in-service education programs both for teachers and administrators.

The superintendents are of the opinion that the improvement of the state departments of education is dependent upon the improvement of professional personnel, which, in turn, depends upon an increase in salary scales and the provision of both pre-service and in-service education programs for state department personnel. Several superintendents indicated that they would like to see USOE give top priority in its use of Title V of ESEA funds to such training projects.

Relationships of State Departments
with USOE

USOE has had a long history of close ties with state departments of education. Some state department personnel who have worked closely with USOE for a long time have indicated that state departments of education constitute the primary reference group for the leadership of USOE. As stated elsewhere, most of the personnel in USOE who were interviewed for this study indicated that effective relationships between state departments and USOE are the key to the success of federal aid to education programs. They feel, as do personnel from state departments of education, that USOE cannot work effectively with all of the school districts of the country. They cite the difficulties of working on desegregation problems when USOE has not been able to work through state departments of education.

USOE appears to be well-equipped to deal with the state departments of education as they are now constituted. It has specialists in state educational programs, several of whom have done some of the most important studies on state school administration in this country. Open lines of communication appear to exist between USOE and state superintendents and state department personnel. Frequent contacts are made, for example, concerning problems related to projects financed directly in the departments and federally funded projects of local school districts. Consultants from USOE are often called upon to assist state department personnel in the interpretation of policies and regulations regarding various federal programs. It is reported that USOE has been very flexible in the administration of Title V programs. Through Title V funds the State Agency Cooperative Branch of USOE has assigned consultants to work in face-to-face relationships with specific state department personnel concerning particular programs. All of these programs have been a favorable stimulus to state departments of education, but they have also had the effect of making state departments of education more highly dependent upon USOE.

State department of education personnel who were interviewed for this study generally felt that desirable working relations with USOE have been established, and that conflicts where they occur are rapidly being overcome. They feel that their departments have already been greatly benefited by the new federal programs, the assistance which they have received from USOE, and the additional personnel they have been able to acquire. However, some believe that the development of regional offices of USOE, the funding of regional laboratories, and the establishment of consortiums of school districts under Title III constitute threats to the future of state departments of education. Some of the school superintendents agree, although most viewed these developments as desirable. Some superintendents stated that USOE is filling a vacuum created by the weaknesses of the state departments and their failure to perform a leadership role.

Some personnel from state departments of education are acutely aware of the needs, problems, and perspectives of school superintendents, and some share the traditional schoolman's fear of centralized control. They appear, however, to feel that this control is exercised to a greater degree over local school districts than over state departments of education. Most state department personnel feel that local autonomy need not be sacrificed while maintaining relationships with the federal government. Because of their relationships with the federal government and the assistance they have received for program improvement, state department personnel were more supportive of categorical aid to education than were local superintendents. On the one hand, they have seen the positive achievements of categorical aid in the public schools, both through NDEA and ESEA programs in which they have been directly involved. On the other hand, they recognize that in a program of general aid, assistance would go directly to school districts, and the only role for the state department of education would be as a distributing agency.

A Future Role in Leadership
and Service

It is too early to assess all the changes which have actually occurred in state departments of education as a result of ESEA programs. An almost universal desire exists among state department of education personnel to improve their services and expand their roles. Most of them see federal programs as giving them the resources and teh opportunities to do so. Most of them also feel that they will obtain assistance from USOE if it continues to focus attention upon their problems, and provides them with additional resources to overcome their problems. If nothing else, the new relationship with the federal government has caused state department personnel to evaluate their programs and become increasingly concerned about their image among school administrators and the general public. An incentive has been created for them to define a more important leadership role, and search for ways and resources through which this can be accomplished.

There has been a lot of glib talk about developing state department leadership for the public schools, but neither this role nor what it implies for the governance of the schools has been well defined. Superintendents want the role to be developed, but they want to have an opportunity to help define what it entails. The spirit of local control of the educational enterprise seemingly still dominates in all of the states. Superintendents want leadership without control. They want services and assistance, and they want a state department of education that is pointing the way on critical issues and absorbing some of the shock of community reactions in educational controversies. But they want their own local school districts to be free to choose directions and determine the degree to which they will follow the leaders. Apparently, they do not fear that the leader may get so far out in front that he loses contact with the followers, but some officials of state departments of education realize that this is a real danger. Distinctions have to be made between the regulatory and the leadership functions of state departments, and these areas cannot be entirely separate.

The superintendents who were interviewed tended to agree that the state departments of education should use their resources to identify major strategic goals for education within the state, and they should provide educators and the public the assistance they need for the accomplishment of these goals. To the superintendents this implies that the leadership role of the state department of education involves both legislative and public relations functions. To a considerable extent, the superintendents reflect the point of view that the definition of goals involves the appraisal of the consensus of the field rather than charting new directions independently of the field. It is apparent that there is a conflict of perspectives between local superintendents and the leadership of state departments of education and that this conflict needs to be resolved.

To superintendents, the emerging leadership role of the state departments has best been demonstrated in the provision of extensive research and information services for the schools. They want the state department to develop data storage and retrieval systems designed to give them information they need about current trends and practices in the schools, as well as statistical information to assist them in local decision-making. Even beyond this, superintendents want the state department to have the resources through which information can be obtained about the best research available on any educational problem and what this research implies for educational practice. Because they realize that they, their principals, and their teachers do not have the skills necessary for the interpretation of much of the research which is available, they want the state departments of education to act as the "intermediary" agent for them, interpreting the research and developing for them the technologies which will enable them to bring about greater congruence between existent knowledge and professional practice. For accomplishing these ends, or some desirable variations of them, the state departments of education face three imperatives which will be difficult to meet. First, it is essential that state departments of education develop methods of working and existing within the political arena which do not interfere with their professional responsibilities. It would be easy to say that the state department of education should be removed from politics, as many superintendents have suggested. But it is neither possible nor desirable for education that it be removed. The state department of education needs to be viewed not only as a political arm of government, but also as a political agency for education within the state. The problem arises from the fact that it is currently viewed more as the political arm of the state government than as a good representative of education before the political agencies of the state.

Superintendents view the political dependency of state departments as one of the most serious obstacles to its professional operation. The key issue of their political dependency is the manner by which state superintendents for public instruction are selected. Most superintendents believe that the state superintendents should be appointed by non-partisan state boards of education, but there are some fears that state boards may become too highly political. Superintendents of one state reported that recent constitutional change made the state superintendency an appointive office, but the board, composed of representatives of a single political party, appointed a state superintendent for patronage reasons. Under the circumstances, these school superintendents view the present functioning of the office as more political than ever.

In the American political ethos, it will be difficult to accomplish what needs to be done. Legislatures will continue to represent various interest groups and the members will keep a wary eye upon their political fortunes. State departments of education will have to advise the governor and the legislature, and, if politics is truly "the art of what is possible," their recommendations will have to reflect some expediency. State school board members and state department officials will continue to be the objects of pressure from various special interest groups. Unfortunately no instrumentality is currently available through which this imperative can be realized. State departments of education must stay in politics, but to operate effectively on a professional level they must be protected from extremes within the political arena. They must be constituted as a meaningful bridge between the operation of the schools, the educational needs of the states, and political decision-making within the states. The structures for accomplishing this end will have to be created.

Second, it is imperative that the state departments of education upgrade the professional stature of their personnel and develop selection procedures and personnel policies which will staff the departments with educators as competent as those now employed in many universities and the largest school districts in the country. State departments should be able to employ educators who are recognized for their specialized knowledge and who can render expert services to school personnel. They need personnel who will be respected for their judgments and in whose recommendations administrators and teachers will have confidence. Superintendents identified three measures that are necessary to accomplish this end: (1) Salaries must be improved to attract and hold qualified individuals in competition with other educational agencies; (2) selection and screening processes, similar to those used in leading universities and the largest school districts, must be developed to identify individuals who have the unique competencies and personalities required for effective performance of their positions; and (3) through USOE and universities, extensive in-service education programs must be developed to retrain and upgrade existing personnel.

Third, it is generally recognized that state departments of education cannot perform their responsibilities adequately if legislatures continue to starve them financially. Money is needed not only to pay competitive salaries, but to extend the range of essential personnel and services available to school districts, to develop improved data processing, storage, and retrieval systems, to extend their research facilities, and to provide funds for professional travel, educational workshops, training scholarships, and other measures designed to enable them to perform their leadership role.

The problems which have kept the state departments of education from being effective have not been entirely resolved. There is still the concern that they may interfere with local control over educational decision-making if they become too strong. There is still the concern that they may force rural areas into consolidation, or in other ways impose professional standards upon a reluctant "lay" public. There is also the fact that already strong educational agencies fear the possibility of losing some of their authority and prestige to state departments of education if these become broader in scope and more competent to render leadership to the field. In large measure, rivalry already exists with universities, and some professors interviewed for this study readily admitted that it was not to the advantage of their institutions that state departments experience a renaissance. Although properly-staffed universities could perform some of the services which state departments of education now provide, there appears to be little if any inclination on the part of professors to do so.

There might also be some concern lest the emerging role of the regional laboratories and the regional offices of USOE overlap with the functions of the state departments of education, drain off resources, and develop publics which will feel it to their own advantage to prevent existing agencies from enlarging their functions.

The success of the state department of education in solving these problems depends upon its ability to devise plans for the coordination of the roles of existing agencies and the delineation of areas of responsibility so that resources can be used in a mutually supportive rather than conflictive fashion. At present, school districts are not receiving maximum benefit from the specialized resources which exist because of the failure among agencies to define roles and responsibilities that mesh and support each other. They fear that if they use resources from other agencies, they will help build the empires of these agencies rather than provide realistically for their own needs. It is certainly reasonable to expect that maximum effectiveness will be achieved only when the agencies and public school administrators commit themselves to cooperative endeavors. R. L. Johns[1] points out that the state department of education is the logical agency to provide a linkage between the various agencies designed to assist school districts in the solution of their problems. Without an effective state department, it is unlikely that such a linkage will take place. There is some likelihood that if state departments do not become effective links between these levels of concern, another agency, such as USOE, will have to come in to fill the gap. It is also possible that a strong state university may do so.

Another difficult problem for state departments of education is to determine whom they represent and which interests they are obligated to promote. The local superintendent wants it to be an instrument of support

---

[1] R. L. Johns. "State Organization and Responsibilities for Education." Edgar L. Morphet and Charles O. Ryan, Eds. *Implications for Education of Prospective Changes in Society.* (Denver: Designing Education for the Future, 1967), pp. 245-266.

for the administration of the public schools. He wants the state department of education to be his representative before the legislature, and he wants it to make available those resources which will assist him in solving his problems without imposing regulatory controls. The state department of education has been criticized in some places, for example, for not having helped administrators work out effective means for negotiating with teachers. However, this raises a significant question as to whether or not the state department of education dares to orient its program toward administrative needs as long as teachers can likewise expect the state department of education to be concerned with their needs and desires.

The public, too, enters into the problem. Citizens seem to want the state department of education to be their "court of last appeal" through which they can secure redress when unfavorable decisions are made on the local level or when dissension with local school officials arises. With increasing public interest in education, there is obviously increasing pressure for the state to develop instrumentalities which are representative of the public concern and which are also capable of dealing professionally and competently with educators who are not always responsible to public desires. It is not simply a matter of protecting the public against malpractice, which is a long recognized obligation of state regulatory agencies, but of providing an actual implementing device for maintaining responsiveness of professional practice to legitimate public claims.

As long as education is primarily a function of the state, the legislature of the state will impose demands and regulations upon the schools. A law-making body must have an administrative arm to carry out its mandates. For public education it creates an agency which it can hold responsible both for fulfilling its requirements and for providing adequate custodianship over the schools. Regulatory functions are inherent in the nature of the state department of education. Leadership may be defined in terms of promoting both public and professional concern about education. Perhaps the state department of education can serve both areas, but the level of diplomacy and of professional and public responsibility required is far beyond the abilities of most state departments today.

To be the kind of agency that is needed to help solve current problems facing education and to point education in the directions in which it will best serve the emerging needs of society, the state department of education must resolve these issues. It is apparent that it is currently in a confused situation and that there is no effective theory by which it can be guided. Not much effort has been expended upon the development of such a theory nor on the practical resolution of the most significant issues which most departments face. Under the circumstances, state departments of education have built dreams of their leadership roles, but with only a few exceptions do they appear to be guided by realistic principles which help them to fulfill the expectations which school superintendents generally have for them. To fulfill these expectations, a general overhaul is needed, and extensive, basic study of their problems and potentials is essential.

5/

Colleges and Universities
as Resources
to Superintendents

Educational administrators look to the colleges and universities for their pre-service preparation. In-service education as well as research nad consultative services are assumed to be resources which are also available from these institutions. Faculty in educational administration from 34 colleges and univeristies geographically distributed throughout the United States were interviewed as one aspect of this study. The interviews focused upon preparatory programs for superintendents, both pre-service and in-service, and upon means through which institutions of higher education serve as resources to superintendents. Superintendents, too, were asked to give their perceptions of colleges and universities as resources for helping to resolve their problems.

The institutions selected were considered to be the major preparatory institutions in the states they served. Several universities were nationally recognized as prestigious insttiutions. Staff interviewed were those having responsibilities for preparation, research, and in-service programs for educational administrators. At a number of institutions arrangements had been made for group interviews in which several staff members responsible for various aspects of the institution's programs participated.

Preparation Programs for
Educational Administrators

Program descriptions

Most colleges and universities offer several levels of preparatory pro-

101

grams. About half offer a Master's Degree program in educational administration. The Master's Degree, in most cases, serves as a minimum program, allowing the holder to qualify for a restricted certificate. In nearly all cases, the master's program is designed for an administrative position less than that of superintendent, usually the principalship. In only a few institutions does the program completed at the master's level fulfill the state certification requirements for superintendents. College and university personnel interviewed feel that more preparation is necessary for the training of superintendents than is available through a master's program. Most institutions offering a master's program in educational administration wish to phase it out, and a number of universities have time tables for doing so.

Programs beyond the Master's Degree but less than the doctorate are available at most institutions. These programs lead to educational specialists' certificates or degrees (going by various names), normally requiring the completion of two years of graduate study or one full year's work beyond the Master's Degree. Educational specialist programs at two institutions require three years of graduate study. Educational specialist programs are not popular, it was reported. Few students select this option in preference to a program leading to a doctorate, even though program planners suspect that many students entering doctoral programs in educational administration actually do not intend to obtain the degree. Individuals tend to drop out as soon as they qualify for certification. Interviewees speculated that candidates select the doctoral program as a means to certification rather than take the specialist route because of the greater flexibility in courses and residence requirements which the doctoral program stipulates.

Only four institutions included in this study do not offer doctorates in educational administration. Two of these institutions are state colleges which, by law, are not permitted to offer the degree. The other two institutions not offering doctorates in educational administration are state universities, one in a sparsely settled state, the other in a populous but geographically small state. Academic regulations which are not professionally relevant were a major factor in the latter university's not offering a doctorate in educational administration. Each of these states has comparatively few school districts.

Not all students entering administrative preparatory programs plan to be superintendents. This is especially true of students in doctoral programs. Some are preparing to be professors or researchers. Students frequently change their emphasis while in the program, shifting their aspirations for positions in school districts to those in colleges or universities.

College and university personnel interviewed were asked, "What is the emphasis in your preparatory program in educational administration —preparation of superintendents, university professors, or researchers?" Only one university indicated that its program has the flexibility to prepare for all three types of positions. Approximately one-half of the programs were designed solely for preparing the practitioner to serve in school districts. One-fourth of the programs provide preparation for both practitioners and professors. Six universities said their programs are designed solely for preparing professors. None of the institutions devotes its efforts exclusively to the development of researchers, although two university programs emphasized preparation of researchers and professors rather than school practitioners.

Program emphasis

Preparation programs tend to be remarkably similar from institution to institution. Most programs require in their professional education sequence a general administration and organization course followed by a series of courses organized around specialized aspects of administration, such as school buildings, school finance, public relations, curriculum, supervision, and personnel management. A few institutions offer courses organized around fragments of the total administrative process, which might serve to synthesize courses previously taken. Courses such as "Administrative Behavior," "Criteria for Decision-Making in Educational Administration," "Administrative Theory," and "Administrative Problems" might afford the opportunity to conceptualize problems and issues in educational administration.

Course titles, alone, provide little reliable information as to whether a preparation program is geared to emphasize techniques or to conceptualize and understand the administrative process. Course titles do tend to define the boundaries of a course. As such, programs having courses with narrow boundaries, emphasizing specialized administrative tasks, limit opportunities for viewing administration as a whole and seeing existing relationships among its parts.

A clue to the emphasis in a preparation program along the technical-conceptual continuum is the extent and nature of practicum experiences the program affords. Approximately one-half of the institutions visited provide extended practicum experiences in at least one of three ways: (1) courses which are essentially field courses, such as "School Surveys,"

(2) experiences integrated into required course offerings, and (3) internships. These courses are designed primarily to develop the technical skills needed by administrators.

The ways in which the behavioral sciences and humanities as foundations for educational administration are included in the preparation program can also provide clues about its technical-conceptual emphasis. These are included in preparation programs in a number of ways: (1) courses taught in the school or college of education in which the focus of the discipline is upon education, e.g., "History of Education," "Philosophy of Education," "Educational Psychology," "Social Foundations;" (2) program requirements for courses offered outside the division of education in the behavioral sciences, philosophy, and humanities; (3) interdisciplinary courses in the professional education sequence; and/or (4) a combination of any or all of the preceding three ways. Most institutions require three foundation courses offered in the division of education: "History and Philosophy of Education," "Educational Psychology," and "Social Foundations," (sometimes called "Educational Sociology"). Regardless of the pattern, approximately two-thirds of the programs require cognate work in the behavioral sciences. The number of required term hours of cognate courses varied from 3 to 30, with most institutions requiring 12 to 15. Most institutions do not specify the exact courses in the behavioral sciences which are to be taken.

Program development

Personnel at a number of institutions, when questioned about program development, said they either had planned or were planning program changes to include more emphasis on the behavioral sciences and more courses having an interdisciplinary approach. In general, they were moving from the technical toward the conceptual in their programs. At three institutions, the individuals interviewed stressed the point that their program emphasis was conceptual rather than technical. One respondent said:

A shift is now taking place in the emphasis in our program. Although it has been somewhat technically oriented as a result of the nature of the personnel who taught in our program, there is now a much greater emphasis upon the conceptual and the disciplinary aspects of school administration. There is a much greater emphasis currently upon theory in our various courses than was formerly the case.... We are moving further and further toward the conceptual.

Some fear was expressed at one institution about the conceptual emphasis of the program.

Our program develops people who are weak in the technical areas of administration. They have difficulty, I am sure, in preparing a school budget. They are conceptually strong, but technically weak.

Respondents identified several forces which influence the curriculum in educational administration. Included among these forces are certification requirements, accrediting agencies, recommendations from AASA, and the studies and developmental activities of the University Council for Educational Administration. Some colleges and universities had made program alterations during recent years. Some interviewees said their curriculum was continually undergoing change. The extensiveness of program changes could not be determined from the data. Perhaps the changes were major or as one university person said, "Program change occurs primarily as individual instructors up-date their offerings."

Several universities that have devoted most of their attention to the preparation of practitioners want to expand their programs to prepare professors of educational administration as well. Most institutions indicated that they want to strengthen their preparatory programs by placing more emphasis on research and the behavioral sciences. Few institutions are actively engaged in curriculum development or in planning major revisions in their programs for preparing educational administrators.

Preparatory programs at most universities were designed to prepare administrators of medium-sized school districts. One university has just completed plans to shift the focus of its program to prepare school administrators for metropolitan cities. One other university is studying possible ways that its curriculum might provide more opportunity to prepare central office personnel for large city schools.

Only one institution indicated that it uses superintendents as a source of information for program development. A one-day conference has been held at this university each year for the past 35 years to obtain specific feedback about selected issues that have implications for the preparatory program. Information about the topic is sent to participants prior to the conference. The conference is opened with a guest expert speaking on the issue. The large group, then, is divided into small groups which discuss implications for administration and preparatory programs. Each small group session is recorded and members of the faculty screen the information for creative and useful ideas. Some of these conferences have been focused upon the preparatory program as a whole.

A number of barriers to program development were reported. Several respondents felt there were too many colleges and universities in the state engaged in administrative preparation. A representative of one state university reported:

> One barrier we have not yet overcome is the large number of institutions in the state engaged in preparatory programs for school administrators. The university's program is the only one requiring a year's residency, and consequently many students would rather go down the road a few miles taking courses as they can get them toward certification rather than follow the university's planned program.

The proliferation of preparatory programs results in a diffused distribution of students and smaller enrollments than are desirable to maintain quality programs. Insufficient student enrollment was reported to be a barrier to the expansion of the curriculum, the employment of sufficient staff to round out staff competencies, and the effective utilization of student interaction. Several respondents reported that departments of educational administration were understaffed, resulting in excessive work loads. Too little time for planning and evaluating programs also prevents curriculum development.

Several colleges and universities have programs designed more for the preparation of principals, curriculum directors, and supervisors, than for superintendents. Faculty at these institutions believe that the route to the superintendency is through promotion from one of these positions. Preparation for superintendents, *per se*, is not their goal. They offer courses, conferences, and in-service activities by which the superintendent may expect to update and broaden his competencies.

In one state, neither of the major universities included in the sample is interested in the general preparation of educational administrators. One of these universities is a private institution primarily interested in the preparation of professors and a lesser number of educational specialists. The other institution is a state university, which is interested in only the top five percent of the student population, who are seeking to become leaders in educational administration. The state colleges thus far have not received approval to provide programs for the preparation of administrators and there is some doubt that they will develop the resources to offer a preparatory program for superintendents. As a result, most superintendents needed in this area are coming from outside of it, and the desires of the present superintendents for in-service education are not being adequately met. The state colleges are cut off from the mainstream of developments in the field of educational administration, since they are not permitted to offer the doctorate, and are not eligible to participate in UCEA activities. Neither are faculty members from the state colleges called frequently to serve as consultants, since most districts prefer to obtain these services from the more prestigious institutions.

Some professors indicated that certification requirements are also sometimes a barrier to program development. In some instances, they are highly prescriptive and do not allow institutions to develop the full programs they deem desirable.

The relationship of the school or college of education to other divisions of the university has a bearing upon program development, especially in those institutions desiring to increase the emphasis on the behavioral sciences and humanities in their programs. Relationships with the behavioral science divisions vary. Most professors of educational administration reported an excellent relationship. Their meaning of "excellent" ranged from being able to arrange for education students to take behavioral science offerings without the necessary prerequisites to having behavioral science faculty members participate in program development activities for educational administrators. A few universities indicated they have behavioral scientists who are interested in the field of educational administration on the faculty of the division of educational administration. One university described its program this way:

> Our program has a totally interdisciplinary focus. The staff in the division of educational administration is interdisciplinary. .... is in sociology. .... has his background in economics. .... has a background in social psychology, and I guess I have a background that ranges over a rather large field. Sixty percent of the faculty in the department of education have degrees outside the field of education. We have ties which are either formal or informal with practically all fields in the university, and particularly with those fields that have anything to do with administration. We are conducting some work with business education in teacher negotiations; we have strong relationships with the law school; we have highly personalized relationships with people in the department of sociology, particularly .... who is very strongly interested in the field of educational administration. The same is true of political science and anthropology.

University personnel interviewed were asked, "How does the university maintain contact with the field and do you have any systematic means of identifying problems and issues facing superintendents?" Most institutions reported they maintain contact with the field through informal communications with former students, consultantships, activities of professional organizations, field service activities, and in-service programs and clinics. Those schools having internships reported this activity as a helpful contact with the field. Two institutions encourage faculty to visit superintendents when they travel about the state. One of these universities reported that more than 500 visits had been made during the past two years. No university admitted to any systematic means of identifying problems and issues faced by superintendents. One interviewee at a university whose faculty had numerous contacts with the field through internships, professional associations, consultantships, and involvement in state-wide improvement program activities, asserted that no systematic program for identifying major problems confronting administrators is needed when there is adequate, constant contact with school administrators.

Research and Field Service in Educational Administration

Inquiry was made concerning research activities in educational administration conducted at the institution. One university reported that a research and development center which conducts research on the social context of educational administration is located on the campus. One other university had a program of research activities carried on under the auspices of several granting agencies. Other than programs at these two institutions, very few research activities are being conducted except by individual staff members in their particular areas of interest. Most institutions provide no released time for faculty engaged in individual research projects.

Approximately half of the universities included in this sample reported they had bureaus of field services. A number of these are all-university bureaus rather than bureaus devoted chiefly to school services. The bureau activities consist primarily of conducting school surveys. Three bureaus are actively engaged in survey activities; however, nearly one-third of the institutions reporting bureaus said their operations are limited to only one or two surveys a year. Very few comprehensive surveys are made to project long range planning. Most survey activities are partial and frequently conducted for information to meet an immediate need or crisis. Typical surveys provide information to the school district about facilities, finance, and curriculum. Two universities maintain bureaus primarily to provide practicum experiences for students. Surveys and other activities by these bureaus are selected carefully, on the basis of the needs of their preparation programs. Several colleges and universities said their bureaus contribute to the financial support of graduate students in their programs. Some universities have phased out their field service bureaus in recent years. Several state universities indicated that they provide surveys as a part of their obligation as state supported institutions. These universities feel that they have continuing service obligations. Other state universities and all private ones felt no such obligation, and professors engaged, if at all, in service activities for the honoraries they received.

Personnel interviewed reported shortage of staff as the reason for their limited research activities and the decrease in field service operations. Faculty time is required for teaching, advising, and guiding doctoral dissertations.

In-service Education of School Administrators

Provisions for in-service education of school administrators was one concern of this study; consequently, inquiry was made to determine what provisions colleges and universities make for the continuing education of superintendents.

Most institutions reported they cooperated with the state administrators' association in planning and offering conferences. These conferences are yearly affairs of short duration, usually one or two days. Conference themes generally focus on a problem or issue currently facing administrators. Also some universities sponsor short conferences on their own campuses. These conferences, for the most part, are not regularly scheduled activities, but are held as the university recognizes an issue and is motivated to be of service. Faculty members at one institution where an annual conference has been held for many years reported their objective was primarily good public relations. One university had a committee of superintendents selected from widely divergent geographic areas of the United States engaged in studying the problems of in-service education of the school administrator.

Workshops, institutes, and clinics were reported by many colleges and universities as summer offerings available to superintendents. These offerings are developed so the superintendent may keep up with latest trends and analyze current problems in the field of administration. One university which has an intern and extern program felt that the two year experience, wherein the university staff follows the administrator in the field, is valuable continuing education. The externs meet ten times during each year for week-end seminars. A multi-disciplinary seminar is also provided during the second year.

Several colleges and universities considered that their advanced graduate courses were the primary in-service education which they provided for school administrators. One institution has experimented with a semester-long in-service education course, entitled "Education Leadership Clinic." The clinic met weekly to explore selected problems currently confronting administrators.

College and university respondents expressed disappointment with the in-service activities they sponsor. They reported generally poor attendance at conferences and workshops. One institution said they held a summer conference on the topic of negotiations for which three national leaders in the field served as consultants; only six superintendents in the state availed themselves of the opportunity to attend. University faculty who sometimes serve as consultants to conferences, institutes, and clinics expressed dissatisfaction with them because of their short duration. Time is generally insufficient to do more than provide an orientation to the problem or topic and, hopefully, to inspire superintendents to explore the ideas further. Seldom is there opportunity to initiate activities designed to develop the technical skills necessary for the superintendent to cope successfully with the problem.

Two state universities reported strong commitment to the university's role of service to the state. Colleges of education in these institutions work closely with their respective state departments, state professional organizations, and school districts in developing programs of in-service, consultantship, and conference activities. No charge is made to school districts utilizing faculty consultant service from these institutions. One of these universities, although strongly committed to service, has been hampered in its activities by shortage of personnel. Activities also were felt to lack a systematic, planned approach to the problems of in-service. The other university, working cooperatively with agencies having the related purpose of in-service, has developed an organized, coordinated and systematic program. The program, which has been in operation for five years, resulted in a state-wide effort to improve the quality of leadership. A theme for the program is developed yearly and is usually an outgrowth of the previous year's activities. Seminars, retreats, and demonstration activities are carried on at the state, regional, and local level. As part of the total effort, the state department of education has made it possible for a limited number of administrators to work toward a doctorate by providing a $4,000 stipend for each student. Twenty superintendents and principals had received these grants during the past two years. However, more superintendents than principals have taken advantage of the program. In the majority of cases, the board of education of the district from which the participant came supplemented the state's stipend with an amount sufficient to equal his full salary.

Respondents from private universities reported that they felt no responsibility for in-service education activities. They believe the in-service education of administrators to be the responsibility of state universities. One interviewee at a state university, however, indicated that he did not believe the in-service education of superintendents was a university responsibility. He said:

> In-service training of administrators is a responsibility of superintendents through their professional association. The university should not have to play another role. The association should look to three major sources of help, the professional association itself, the university, and the state department of education in developing in-service programs.

Superintendents' Views of Colleges and Universities as Resources

Mixed attitudes were expressed by superintendents about the adequacy of preparation programs for school administrators. One group felt that colleges and universities were preparing administrators as well as could be expected and that much of the learning had to be acquired through experience on the job. Another group believed that much of what was taught in preparatory programs was obsolete. Some felt that there were gaps in their preparation, but there were divergent opinions as to what was missing in preparatory programs. About half of those criticizing shortages in their preparation wanted more emphasis upon conceptualization. They felt they could benefit from the perspectives of the behavioral scientists in the analysis of their problems. They wanted to be able to see the "big picture." Another group felt short-changed in some of the technical skills. They would include more emphasis on personnel and organizational management skills. They felt a need to be able to work effectively in the local, state and national political arena where many of the issues affecting schools were hammered out. Several administrators were disturbed that the Universities did not consult with the practitioner about the preparatory curriculum.

Concern was expressed about the quality of faculty. Some superintendents saw university faculties as being staffed by too many former superintendents who "have retreated to the university." Another group of superintendents was concerned about the background experiences of university staff. "Too many of them have never been superintendents and don't know the realities of the job. They are too theoretically oriented." Concern was also expressed about faculty members, who— even though they may previously have been superintendents—have been associated with the university for so long that they have lost contact with the problems of the field. Several recommended that college faculty should be forced back into the field periodically so they can maintain a proper perspective.

Some administrators were concerned about the increasing gap between university professors and school districts. There was, formerly, a closer relationship than exists at present. One superintendent expressed it this way:

> Colleges and universities are not as helpful as they were ten or fifteen years ago. They have federal contracts and they are not as close to superintendents as they once were. We really don't see them unless they are running a research program in our area. We're a middle-class white district and we're not of interest to universities as an experimental group. We see university people as consultants only and sometimes when we are taking over their class when they're going away. They are available to call if you are in trouble that is, if you can catch them. They are frequently in Washington or somewhere else.

A large number of administrators felt colleges and universities were not assuming the leadership role in school administration. One superintendent believed:

> Colleges are selling us short. They should be the protectors of the concepts undergirding education. They should be constantly evaluating new proposals in terms of what they will do to the basic patterns of education. They should be analyzing what education is all about, what it stands for. They are not sufficiently sensitive to their responsibility for questioning legislation and proposed solutions to problems.

Superintendents interviewed tended to seek out prestigious institutions for administrative consultant services without too much regard for state boundaries or the nearness of the institution to the school district. This was particularly noted in the Northeastern and Western sections of the nation. College and university bureaus of field services were valued for their surveys by about one-third of the superintendents. Here, again, if a comprehensive survey were required, school districts contracted with prestigious institutions. Superintendents whose districts belong to school study councils felt them to be valuable resources. Study council reports of research and their newsletters were viewed as being very helpful. A number of superintendents indicated that local colleges and universities expressed willingness to be helpful, but did not have the resources to help them with administrative problems.

Superintendents' opinions varied concerning the value of conferences and workshops sponsored by colleges and universities. A large group thought they were excellent, providing inspiration and keeping them abreast of latest developments. Other superintendents felt the conferences and workshops focused on problems and issues that were "after the fact," dealing with topics that might have been more relevant at an earlier time. Some also thought the university conferences were too theoretically oriented, utilizing consultants who were not closely enough associated with the realities of school administration. Superintendents from urban school districts reported that college and university preparatory programs, conferences, and in-service activities did not meet the needs of city school administrators.

Many superintendents expressed the same concern about conferences as college and university faculty indicated, that the conferences were too short to provide more than a brief orientation to a problem under consideration. At the same time superintendents said they did not know how they could be away from their jobs any longer, if the length of conferences was extended.

Summary

In spite of significant improvements during the past 15 years, it is apparent that universities face many unresolved problems relative to their roles in the preparation of educational administrators and the development of programs to assist them. It is also apparent that superintendents feel that improvements are needed in preparatory, in-service education, and research and service programs currently provided.

The larger universities appear to be indecisive as to what their major emphasis should be. Many are directing their efforts increasingly toward the preparation of professors of educational administration rather than toward the improvement of programs for practicing school administrators. They have not solved the issue of whether or not they can develop adequate programs for the preparation of professors without first having well-rounded administrative certification programs.

Few universities seem actually to have developed a balanced program for administrators in which all required skills and knowledge receive proper emphasis. Some emphasize technical skills, and others, admittedly, hope to become increasingly less technical as greater emphasis is placed upon the conceptual. The result of the failure to achieve balance is the neglect of certain areas of concern for superintendents, while other facets of the preparation are over-emphasized.

Almost all programs now include some emphasis upon the study of the behavioral sciences as a part of the administrative preparation program, but there is a scarcity of consistent programs with well-developed rationales for the use of behavioral sciences in preparing administrators for the achievement of specified goals.

Some institutions are obviously engaging in administrative preparatory programs without the number or quality of professors essential to provide for the range of skill and knowledge needed by the practicing superintendents. Superintendents noted with some feeling that professors were not always aware of the contemporary problems of the field, nor did universities always provide the range of resources they could use to improve their practice or to resolve issues confronting their school districts.

In practically all of the mature professions, preparatory institutions maintain considerable resources for the continuing educational needs of practitioners throughout their careers. In educational administration, it seems that little is being done in the in-service education of superintendents, and even less is done well.

To fulfill their responsibilities toward superintendents whom they have trained and to supply the schools with administrators who can deal effectively with all the complex educational problems confronting today's schools, universities will have to make some major adjustments. Discussion of some of these adjustments will be reserved for the final chapter.

6/

Regional Educational Laboratories
and Their Services
to Superintendents

Since 1954, the Cooperative Research Act has supported educational research by colleges, universities, and state educational agencies. In 1965, Title IV of the Elementary and Secondary Education Act extended the authority of the Cooperative Research Act so that non-profit corporations could be formed to serve self-defined areas or regions of the nation to improve the educational system. It was under this provision that the regional educational laboratories were established. The regional approach to educational improvement affords opportunity for an attack on common, pressing problems characterizing the region.

These newly created agencies have the opportunity to utilize all necessary and appropriate resources in a cooperative approach toward the solution of regional educational problems. Initially, each laboratory has been charged with the responsibility of assessing the educational needs and interests of its region, developing an organizational structure, and establishing priorities and initial program activities to meet the identified needs.

Describing the purposes of the regional educational laboratories, President Johnson said:

> These laboratories constitute a major new kind of institution to achieve rapid increases in educational quality on a mass scale. . . . The laboratories should be large and significant enterprises, equal in size and scope to the major tasks they seek to accomplish. They ought to be conceived as comparable in their way to the large-scale laboratories of the defense or atomic energy establishments. Nothing less will do. Their missions

115

are equally important. . . . I look to these laboratories to stress putting into practice what we already know. The increase of knowledge through research must proceed at a rapid pace. But we have an even greater obligation to overcome the lag between discovery and use, and to convert the results of years of research into application in the classroom. This process will be speeded by establishment of extensive experimental schools and pilot projects showing educational innovations in real situations that can be seen and understood by administrators, teachers and school boards.

Congress had authorized funds for 20 of these regional laboratories at the time data were gathered for this study. Twelve of the laboratories were in the first year of operation, while eight were in the developmental stage.

Regional educational laboratories were included in this study to determine if they can and do serve as resources to superintendents in the identification, clarification, and solution of educational issues and problems. Six laboratories were visited by members of the research team; others were contacted by correspondence or reviewed by reference to brochures and progress reports. In addition, superintendents were interviewed on the subject of regional laboratories and their reactions were recorded.

Focus or Thrust of Regional Laboratories

An attempt was made to determine the major thrusts of the regional educational laboratories to see how their activities added to the resources available to school administrators. Responses by laboratories to the inquiry, "What are your major objectives?" varied considerably. There was some apparent confusion between objectives and projects. To give the flavor of the responses, a few are listed below:

> To determine how educational change can be brought about. We are not so much interested in a specific change, as such, but the *processes* which lead to desirable educational change. We hope to find processes which are effective and exportable from one setting to another.

> To ease the transition from school to the world of work.

> To advance the quest for quality integrated education within urban school districts through the conduct of both applied and basic social scientific and educational research.

> To reduce educational deprivation.

To utilize and combine resources of agencies such as state education agencies, colleges and universities, school districts, and other related agencies in applying the results of research to educational processes. We hope (1) to decrease the time lag between research and practice, (2) to apply research findings, (3) to apply technical developments, and (4) to encourage innovation.

To coordinate and use existing resources and serve as a model to develop, disseminate, and demonstrate promising educational practices.

To improve the way students learn in a setting characterized by two problems: (1) sparse population and isolated communities, and (2) urban areas with slum schools and *de facto* segregation.

Differences in focus or thrust from laboratory to laboratory were evident, as the above statements reveal. In fact, one of the laboratory directors said, "One of the major problems in setting up the laboratory was trying to determine its role."

Exploration of the projects planned or underway revealed even further diversity, although the categories of activities were similar. One laboratory spelled out its categories of activities as follows:

Surveying needs—This activity concerns the sampling of students, teachers, principals, or others, to determine the frequency of certain needs and problems.

Problem formulation—This is a very important research and development activity relating to definition of problems. Needs are often expressed in "raw" form, and must be further interpreted and definitely formulated in order to determine appropriate courses of action. The latter sometimes turn out to be other than research or development activities.

Individual research studies—New ideas often begin in relatively restricted form. Research activities related to school problems may be carried out by individual students or with small groups. The findings of such investigations can be of tremendous importance, but are typically not immediately applicable to school practices.

Pilot studies—Such studies are usually carried out to test the feasibility of a new idea, technique, or set of materials in a school setting or with particular kinds of students. Typically, they are restricted in scope or applicability, and suggest the requirements for more comprehensive evaluation.

Development—A new technique, a new system for teaching, a new set of materials, a new audio-visual aid, or other product may be developed. Often development follows an initial pilot study. Developing curricular materials is a fairly substantial kind of research effort. Newly developed materials and techniques should be accompanied by concurrently developed evaluation methods.

Field testing—Materials and techniques that are developed need to be field tested in typical schools or groups of schools. Usually, teacher training in the use of new materials or techniques needs to be planned as part of this kind of activity. Evaluation is an essential feature.

Demonstration—A demonstration usually follows field testing. Its purpose is to show to others what has been accomplished, in order to encourage utilization. Education of teachers and others typically forms a part of this kind of activity.

Most laboratories plan to engage in the entire spectrum of research and development activities, from problem identification to implementation. At the present time, however, projects tend to emphasize dissemination, development, and implementation activities, and some curriculum development is underway. Projects to determine and test technological applications are also receiving emphasis, and demonstration centers are being established to show promising innovations. Compilations of talent, resources, and materials are being made to support laboratory activities. Some curriculum developments are being evaluated and research designs are being utilized to determine the effectiveness of the projects the laboratories are implementing. Data are also being gathered by laboratories to determine needs and frequency of problems. Also some research is being done by individuals or small groups, which is considered important for pointing future directions, rather than for its immediate applicability. Since teacher education, both in-service and pre-service, is tied to program improvements sought by the laboratories most of them have projects related to teacher preparation.

A recent analysis of regional laboratories revealed the same findings as this study:

> ...one becomes conscious of the considerable diversity among the labs in structure, program, and design. Program diversity includes: a focus upon a single problem, broadly treated, such as cultural deprivation; a detailed and sophisticated design for effective dissemination and innovation of the program and process of the single school; teacher education in which student teachers view video tapes of their classroom performance; a vast array of unrelated individual projects; an information clearinghouse function; and an evaluation and field testing function for new instructional media.[1]

While there is considerable diversity among the stated purposes and specific activities of the various regional laboratories, perhaps this is intentional. Regional educational laboratories were given considerable

---

[1] Richard I. Miller, "Regional Educational Laboratories," *Phi Delta Kappan*, 48:4 (December, 1966), p. 145.

flexibility. The April, 1965 issue of *American Education*, published by USOE stated:

There would be no rigid formula—no magic combination of ingredients —that would have to go into every laboratory. Needs and resources of each region would vary, and those setting up lab programs would come with individual solutions to their individual area problems. . . . They would conduct research, develop the results into forms that can be used in the classrooms, continually test and retest these new forms, train teachers in their use, and make them available to local school systems.[2]

Regional Laboratories as a Service

to Superintendents

Regional laboratory activities are programmatic. This means that individual, unsolicited proposals from the field, if accepted at all, will need to find their place within programs designed to reflect regional needs. Laboratories are not funding agencies, although they assume full expense for most projects carried out in the selected school districts where they are implementing programs. Many laboratories do plan, however, to help school districts design and evaluate programs and locate financial support for them. In most cases, consultant services are not directly available from the laboratory, unless the school is one which the laboratory has identified for carrying on a project. Most laboratories are anxious to help schools in the development and evaluation of proposals for ESEA Titles I and III funds.

Most laboratory activities appear to be aimed at the instructional level and at the classroom teacher; however, within the focus of some individual laboratories there are specific projects which relate more directly to the problems of educational administrators. The Southwest Cooperative Educational Laboratory has a program aimed at strengthening of school-community relations and community support for education. Studies of the relationship between boards of education and the communities will be reviewed and definitions established. The laboratory plans to hold institutes at which school board members, administrators, and other interested individuals will consider the findings of research.

One project of particular interest to school administrators is an administrative planning system developed by the Southwest Regional Laboratory. Population growth and pupil mobility, characteristic of the South-

---

2 ". . . The First Work of These Times," American Education, 1:4, (April, 1965), p. 20.

west, compel school administrators to make frequent changes in space, staff, and equipment. Lead time needed for school construction and staffing has increased tremendously, forcing administrators to make complex planning decisions years in advance and on the basis of fragmentary information. This project will develop and install an effective administrative planning system in a number of the region's school districts.

The Center for Urban Education in New York City plans to study the effect of a union contract on the principal's leadership and the educational process in urban schools. This laboratory also has contracted with a number of school districts to study problems of integration in the school district. Teams of social scientists and educators go to the contracting district to study the situation and make recommendations.

Most of the regional laboratories have developed procedures to identify the educational problems in the geographic area served, but they apparently made no distinction between educational problems characterizing the region and problems and issues confronting superintendents. Two laboratory interviewees did make a distinction. One responded:

> No attempt will be made (to identify significant problems facing superintendents); there has been no expressed need to do so. A number of professors of educational administration and superintendents have been on our planning committee, but none has indicated this should be an area in which the laboratory should concentrate its efforts.

The second regional laboratory making the distinction between "educational problems" and "problems and issues facing superintendents" did ask superintendents as a group to identify their own needs. Superintendents identified five areas in which they needed help: (1) upgrading instructional programs, (2) gaining approval of federal projects, (3) planning a program designed to facilitate integration, (4) educating school board members, and (5) securing assistance in legal affairs.

One might question the distinction made here between educational problems of a region and problems and issues facing school superintendents. Are these not the same? To be sure, the two sets of problems are over-lapping, but they are separate when they are considered from the standpoint of role. The superintendent perceives his problems in relation to the multiple roles he plays. One role is that of instructional leader of the school. The activities he pursues in filling this role depend upon the size and organization of his district. In a small district, the superintendent may be very close to and involved in activities designed to increase instructional effectiveness. He may be active in curriculum development; in selection of books, materials, and equipment; and in selection and supervision of personnel. As the school district increases in size and organizational complexity, however, the superintendent's activities may become removed from direct involvement in these activities. Other staff members then direct instructional improvement activities, while the superintendent seeks community support and increased financial resources, struggles with problems of urbanization, integration, negotiations, federal support, and a multitude of other social issues. Under these circumstances the superintendent's role, itself, becomes clouded. Other personnel within the organization tend to view educational problems in terms of their perception of their roles. Outside agencies may not recognize the distinction between problems and issues of school superintendents and educational problems and it is evident from the responses to the question about identifying significant problems of superintendents, that most regional educational laboratory personnel do not.

The distinction being made here is useful to this study primarily because the study is designed to identify problems and issues facing superintendents and to determine resources available to them in resolving these problems. The idea that regional laboratories *should* be or were *intended* to be set up as services to superintendents, as such, is not in question. The question *is* do laboratories serve as a resource to the superintendent regardless of their *raison d'être*.

Since laboratory activities are geared primarily toward instruction and the classroom teacher, the superintendent is likely to perceive the laboratory as a helpful resource to the extent that he is directly involved with instructional improvement. For this reason, the problems which laboratories attempt to resolve may be closer to the small city and rural superintendent than to the superintendent of the larger urban district.

Superintendents' Perceptions of the
Regional Laboratories

By and large, administrators interviewed were optimistic that the regional educational laboratories would benefit the school districts of the region they serve. It was evident, however, that approximately one-third of the superintendents were not knowledgeable of the concept or workings of the regional laboratory, and they did not know the focus of the laboratory which served their region. Even though the original concept was to place resources closer to the schools of the nation, the laboratories are to many superintendents remote structures superimposed over the schools and other educational agencies and located outside of the formal hierarchy of established constituted educational agencies. Consequently, they are not highly visible as sources of help. The very newness of the laboratories may be the immediate reason for this apparent remoteness. Even though most laboratories have circulated information through brochures and newsletters, these media appear to be less effective than one might hope. One possible explanation might be that the superintendent receives so many materials of this type that he simply does not give any of them close attention.

The optimism expressed by knowledgeable superintendents for the regional laboratories seemed to be based upon the idea that the laboratories may become the means through which the resources of all educational agencies in the region for research and development might be pooled and coordinated. They also suggested that regional laboratories develop central foci and coordinated thrusts, using not only their own resources but also those of colleges and universities, state departments of education, and local school districts. Superintendents felt that such coordinated efforts offer promise of higher levels of productivity than is currently the case when each agency develops its independent program and direction. They also felt that since the regional laboratories operate outside of the formally established structure, they will have greater flexibility than universities, state departments of education, or school districts.

Superintendents' desires for the regional laboratories were numerous. Many expressed the hope that laboratories not only serve to collect, summarize, and disseminate research findings and reviews of educational developments, but that they will assist superintendents to translate research studies into educational practice. They foresaw the setting up of demonstration and in-service education centers where experimental practices could be observed and studied, as a promising and valuable laboratory activity. Evaluation of curricular and organizational innovations that individual schools had underway was mentioned frequently, as an activity in which regional laboratories should engage. Other activities suggested by individual superintendents included setting up a data bank with data collected from many sources, experimenting with ideas and projects that an individual school district cannot afford to undertake, surveying individual districts for problems and pointing up possible solutions, helping with proposals for Titles I and III projects, and evaluating funded projects carried on in the school district.

Not all superintendents saw the regional laboratories in positive terms. Many, even though generally supportive, expressed some fear that laboratory activities might not be realistically oriented to educational practice. Several expressed concern that the size of the regions tended to be too large to allow effective service to any particular district. The larger the region, and the more diverse the problems faced by schools, the less will be the opportunity for an individual school district to benefit from the laboratory's activities and the more difficult will be the task of gaining cooperation of the participating institutions of several states.

One superintendent was very negative in his reaction to the laboratories. He said:

> The regional laboratory has taken about sixteen days of my time. At the moment I see the direction they are taking as having little or no value to my school district. It's the same old people talking about the same old things only under a new structure. They are putting a lot of money into raising the same questions we have been raising for a long time, but we haven't done anything very significant about them. Even when we have found out things, we haven't applied them to our schools. The laboratory is not doing the frontier thinking that we expected. Their potential is great, but the probability is not.

Several other superintendents commented that the success of the regional laboratories is directly related to the quality of staff that they employ. They were particularly concerned that the laboratories might become dominated by basic research-oriented staff who lack familiarity with the operating problems of the public schools. The superintendent who made the statement quoted above felt that this was happening in the laboratory which served his area. Other superintendents were less critical because they felt the laboratory staffs in their regions possessed outstanding competence.

One superintendent was concerned about the regional laboratories because he regarded them as one more level of control or influence superimposed upon the schools, and whose role is not entirely clear in the total organizational system of the local through the federal levels. He expressed a feeling that the laboratory was another example of organizational fragmentation which dissipates time and resources vital to education. He said:

> The lab ought to be part of an organizational structure of the U. S. Office of Education, having four levels: local, regional, state, and national. The lab could be part of the mainstream. We need more structure to improve what we are doing. It seems there is no accountability anywhere when we get so many fragmented programs such as this one.

Two respondents, each from different state departments of education, also expressed some apprehension as to the proper place of the regional laboratories in the total structure of education.

Concern about the relationship of Title I funds and the regional laboratories was expressed by one administrator.

> I think the lab could handle all research under Title I. If the research could be consolidated, I think we could get something accomplished. Right now I'm fairly certain that other districts are doing many of the same things we are. This makes for many small projects, and I have a hunch that very little will be accomplished. I think the labs could avoid duplication, could get the staff and equipment necessary to do a good job and really get somewhere. This will take a large staff, but local districts don't have adequate staff either. To do research it takes trained people.

Barriers in Implementation of Laboratory Operations

Laboratory personnel were interviewed about the barriers they encounter in implementing their programs. In general, barriers appeared to be minimal. In most cases the laboratories have received the support and cooperation of school districts in their regions. School districts, for the most part, appeared to laboratory personnel to be anxious to participate in laboratory projects. Several laboratories reported that they had had more volunteers for participation in the various projects than they could utilize. However, two laboratories indicated some difficulty in obtaining support from school districts. One director said, "At the present time we do not have adequate channels of communication with administrators." The purpose of the laboratories is to improve the quality of education in the schools. From the point of view of the superintendent of schools, there is no other function which the laboratories can realistically serve, but they cannot expect to function effectively without the cooperation and support of the public schools.

Two laboratories, both in the developmental or planning stage, reported that they were having difficulties establishing what their roles were to be. The laboratory staff, in each instance, appeared to have some rather definite conceptions of what the laboratories should be doing, but their executive boards did not agree with them. This type of conflict exemplifies one of the most severe difficulties in the operation of the laboratories. Executive boards are appointed or elected to represent a wide range of educational agencies within the region, and they bring to the board diverse conceptions of what the laboratories should be doing and how the laboratories can relate to the programs of the agencies which they represent. These difficulties with role perceptions and reference groups add to the laboratory's inability to identify acceptable programs. Further difficulties may arise. Members of the executive boards have commitments to the agencies which they represent and not necessarily to the regional laboratories, unless the latter serve their purposes.

Generally, laboratory personnel did not consider scarcity of funds a barrier to their activities. However, during the time that data were being gathered for this study, news was received that allocations of federal funds for regional laboratories were much smaller than anticipated by laboratory personnel. In some instances, the resulting budgetary reductions tended to limit the scope of projects planned. Some concern was expressed because commitments had already been made to school districts, and directors feared that a cancellation of projects would impair the development of wholesome working relationships with school districts.

Most of the directors of the laboratories saw USOE in a favorable light, and communication channels with USOE were generally open. Some processing difficulties had been encountered, and one laboratory director indicated that before he could get approval for proceeding with his program he had "to deal with five different coordinators" from USOE. One director still finds himself at odds with personnel from USOE over the general goals of the laboratory. He said the difficulty seemed to be whether,

> ...the U. S. Office is going to let the staff of the regional lab develop its own operation based on the best research evidence known to the staff members, or according to what the U. S. Office staff wants. The laboratory staff wants a maximum degree of openness, a flexibility to respond to the needs of the region as they are determined through our assessment procedures. However, the U. S. Office is pressing for rigidity, specifics, evaluation, etc.

Summary

Since the regional educational laboratories are a newly created invention, it is too early to determine how effectively they will accomplish their purposes. Superintendents were generally optimistic concerning their potential, and although some fears were expressed about their emerging activities, these fears do not appear to be wholly justified. The emphases in the most well-developed programs are clearly upon applied research, development, demonstration, and in-service education projects from which the schools will directly benefit.

The regional laboratories appear to be remote from the school districts, and most of them have some problems communicating information about their activities to school districts and other educational agencies. The fact that approximately one-third of the superintendents interviewed knew nothing about the focus or thrust of the laboratory serving their region may be due to the newness of the laboratories and their need to concentrate upon getting their projects under way. It may also be due to the fact that establishing such communication channels has not as yet been given a very high priority, and the techniques employed are not sufficient. Before superintendents can see the laboratories as having much relevance for them in the solution of their problems or the improvement of their instructional programs, they will have to feel that they are more a part of the laboratories, that the laboratories exist to assist the school districts of the region, and that they are being kept adequately informed of what the laboratories are doing.

Much concern was expressed about the relatively large geographical areas served by each of the laboratories and the place of the laboratories in the total structure of the educational system. The issues appear to be worthy of consideration, even though they were expressed by only a few. There was a feeling that the region served was too large and that the laboratory, as an "extra-legal" agency, further fragmented the field of education and usurped resources which could better be used within the existing structures. Some superintendents and several state department of education officials felt that the regional laboratories were engaging in activities which overlapped with those of existing agencies. They said that they were now having to deal with yet another agency which had "its own axe to grind" and which demanded time and effort from the district.

This group saw the cooperative ventures among school districts, presently funded under Title III of ESEA, as more readily meeting their needs, and they would prefer to see these Title III programs supported with the money now going into the regional laboratories.

On the positive side, other administrators considered the fact that the regional laboratories were outside the traditional structure as a distinct advantage, since this freed them from any regulatory functions and gave them flexibility to attack problems with fresh conceptions, which existing agencies did not have. They also maintained that the laboratories were coordinating their activities with those established in school districts under both Title I and Title III funds.

Laboratory directors feel that they can operate effectively throughout the region since the problems upon which they are working are limited, and they will be able to maintain their focus within these bounds. They generally do not see the laboratories as just service agencies to the schools, at least not in the sense that services are now provided by state departments of education or university bureaus of school services. Laboratory personnel are confident that they can be of great help by encouraging and evaluating proposals for the funds available from ESEA or other sources, as well as in mounting programs within the schools in relation to their major emphasis.

The attention of this study was focused on regional educational laboratories to determine their potential value in assisting administrators to deal with their problems. If the emerging trends are realized, it would seem that superintendents can expect a great deal of assistance from regional laboratories on instructional problems. Most of the laboratories, if not all, are geared to the study of instructional problems and the development of projects in instructional areas. For problems faced by the superintendent outside of the realm of instruction, except for a very few projects under consideration by one or two laboratories, the superintendent cannot expect much assistance from the regional laboratories. He will still have to look to other agencies for the resources he needs.

7 /

Summary
and
Conclusions

Problems of Superintendents

The re-discovery of the importance of education is one of the salient characteristics of the age. At one time in the history of mankind, education was considered a luxury for the delight and edification of the aristocracy. At another time it was, as well, a means of education for the professions and a preparation for power of the ruling classes. Today it is an essential instrument for the realization of all of the legitimate purposes of all of the people. It is in this context that both educators and citizens must review the current status of their educational enterprises and define ways to improve them.

There were few surprises in the perceptions which superintendents voiced concerning their problems. They were asked to express themselves forthrightly, and seemingly they did so. Except for specific details, the problems were very much as generally reported in both the professional and popular press.

The fact that is both surprising and disheartening is that there is so much ready analysis about the problems of school administrators but so little practical assistance rendered by those who could offer aid. More than a decade ago, the American Association of School Administrators wrote of the superintendency:

> Born of tensions, the role of the superintendent continues to be modified by them. As did his predecessors, today's superintendent becomes the

128

focal point of severe and conflicting demands upon the schools. He will do well to realize that today's superintendency will be further modified by these pressures just as it has been reshaped continuously in the past.[1]

The statement cannot be debated, but not even the American Association of School Administrators, itself, has risen to the challenge that is implied in it.

Cultural and social trends affecting the superintendency

A pluralistic society in the throes of transition combines a curious dependency upon the traditional with an unsystematic and almost frantic searching for innovation. Our society is preoccupied with change and innovation, but it is difficult to predict the specific consequences of some of its efforts. Vague notions of societal goals are implicit in many of the political trends of the day, but interpretations of what these mean are as various as the programs which gain the support of different interest groups. The growing emphasis upon education as an instrument for the achievement of social goals—as in the desegregation cases and the war on poverty—has placed the superintendent of schools at the focal point of much of the indecision, the searching for the new, and the clinging to the established order.

Americans seem both to distrust their political leaders and to maintain a "superman" complex for them. The public insists upon increasing provisions for checks against the authority of their leaders; at the same time the leaders are expected to come up with the "answers" which others have failed to find. The superintendent is expected to have solutions to all critical problems, regardless of the state of educational technology or the ability of the American people to specify their aspirations.

The educators are not without blame in this situation. For decades, and with a sort of pollyanna-ish naiveté, educators have been trying to convince the public that education is the solution to its problems. Seemingly, the public believes that education "is good for children." It has underwritten the costs of education as an evidence of goodwill toward the young and of hopefulness toward the future. In times of stress, public interest in education has increased, and expectations for the schools have been high.

Faced with the manifold trauma of the post-World War II years, Americans have had to re-evaluate the schools and their services to society.

---

[1] American Association of School Administrators. *The American School Superintendency.* Thirtieth Yearbook. (Washington, D. C.: The American Association of School Administrators, 1952), p. 39.

The persistence of the cold war, the advent of modern technology, the discovery of manpower shortages in technological and scientific fields, the expansion of needs for professional services of all sorts and the discovery of major discontinuities and incongruities between our social dogmas and our political, social, and economic practices—all have produced an awareness that more emphasis must be placed upon education, and greater attention paid to realistic goals and the effectiveness of the schools in achieving them. No longer can the American society afford an educational program which is merely nice to children.

Superintendents perceive that social change is catching up with the schools, and the public is now too well informed and too much concerned to be satisfied with glittering generalities. Since the position of the superintendent is particularly the link between the schools and the broader society, it is natural that both the community and the professional staff should look to his leadership. Faced with such expectations, the superintendent can emerge either as the hero for meretorious decisions or the scapegoat for unresolved ills. By either evaluation, it is evident that the superintendency has become an increasingly unstable position in American society.

The primary concern here is the fact that education cannot be viewed apart from its context; similarly, the problems of the superintendent cannot be viewed apart from the social issues and trends from which they rise. The problems reported as the foremost concerns of superintendents appear to stem from six currents which are coursing through American society today. At this point, we can only suggest how these problems are related to these currents. Much more needs to be done to analyze them fully and determine their implications for education.

(1) *Revolt against Paternalism.* Practically all governmental, industrial, and educational organizations are based upon a hierarchical model in which authority flows from a central position through the remaining levels of operations. The occupant of one position has authority and decision-making responsibility over others who are subordinate to him.

Today, there is a massive effort among many groups of individuals to change this paternalistic administration of group life and to develop one which diffuses responsibility for decision-making among those individuals who are affected by the decisions. The civil rights movement the emergence of broader participation in political and social affairs, the revolt against minority group disenfranchisement, the agitation against draft laws, the concern about economic dispossession, the popular demand for complete knowledge of all governmental operations, the demand that leaders keep in communication with their followers, the student unrest—all are evidence of the fact that larger numbers of citizens refuse to acquiesce meekly to those in authority without careful scrutiny, and without an opportunity to participate in the deliberations.

The emerging teacher militancy is one of the most significant ways in which this trend affects educational administration. Characteristically, superintendents and school boards have made decisions for teachers with the expectations that teachers would be grateful for the generosities bestowed upon them. A newer breed of teachers refuses to accept as benevolent the paternalism of administrators or of public governing boards. Although a large percentage of the teachers apparently have no direct involvement in the movement, they have tacitly given their support to militant organizations and, on the local level, to the more verbal and aggressive leaders.

Although superintendents charge that teachers are primarily concerned with economic benefits, the range of problems involved in bargaining agreements clearly shows that they insist upon having a voice in decisions on a broad range of topics relating to curriculum, discipline, teacher roles, public relations policies, personnel policies, educational change and innovation as well as both to conditions of work and economic benefits.

These concerns of teachers should not come as a surprise to administrators. As the superintendents clearly indicated, they are victims of their own efforts to upgrade the teaching profession. It was administrators who built the teachers' organizations which have become powerful forces through which teachers can now present their requests. It was the administrators, too, who recognized that the improvement of the quality of education demanded a higher level of professionalism among teachers. They encouraged, for the most part, higher certification standards and greater emphasis upon obtaining advanced degrees and in-service education credits.

Before World War II the average teacher in this country lacked a bachelor's degree. Most came from teachers colleges. There were few men in the profession. Teaching was an intermediary occupation between termination of formal education and entry into one's life-long career. Today, the situation has changed. The majority of teachers have worked beyond the bachelor's degree. Increasing numbers come from universities with liberal arts majors. More men are entering the field, and more teachers hope to make teaching their life work.

By any standards, teaching today has become more professionalized.

The average teacher is more competent to make professional judgments. The average teacher now has educational qualifications which are frequently equivalent to those of the administrator. Increasing numbers of teachers have the training and qualifications necessary to make professional decisions which affect the proper education of children. As a consequence, there are many teachers who feel that they have a proprietary interest in their jobs and that the quality of education in the district will be enhanced through their participation in all levels of decision-making related to the instructional program.

The advent of strong teacher action to support their demands has caught the administrator short in several ways. Ideologically, relatively few administrators appear to be prepared to deal with this new phenomenon. They have grown accustomed to their paternalistic role in the school system and expect the passive compliance of the teachers as evidence of professional interest and conduct. They do not hesitate to express some of the clichés about teaching. ("The greatest rewards for teachers come from service, not salary!") which have long kept teachers in a subordinate position and constrained from raising questions about administrative decisions, be they benevolent or repressive.

On this level, management in education is considerably behind industry, which in a little more than 30 years has come to accept unionism as an instrument for protecting the workers' proprietary interest in their jobs. The majority of administrators do not seem to be prepared to make the shifts necessary to democratize the school organization and to develop a rationale which recognizes the right and the obligation of teachers to participate in professional decision-making. A few leaders among superintendents find it possible to accommodate their perspectives to the newer demands, but many, if not most, superintendents, adopt the traditional attitudes of school boards, which view teacher demands for involvement in decision-making as a threat to their own domination over school policies.

Even if superintendents want to deal effectively with teacher groups in the new fashion, they find virtually no established technology or experience in education which they can use as guides for establishing procedures for negotiations, grievance committees, consultative management, and group decision-making.

Teacher organizations are prepared to utilize the experiences of labor organizations and effective teacher associations in other countries. They use their extensive resources to formulate strategies for teachers' committees and to give teachers the "in-service" training they need for militant action. Superintendents have no such support behind them. Their professional organizations seem to be taking the side of the teachers rather than offering positive and useful aids for administrators, who need both to define their roles and discover operating principles for dealing with this new situation.

In this new situation, administrators cannot define their roles. They have been the representatives of teachers before the boards and have long felt that the teaching profession is a primary reference group for them. Now the teachers demand to represent themselves before the boards, and in some states legislation has been adopted making it mandatory for boards and superintendents to accord them this privilege. Faced with the conflict inherent in negotiations, the school boards are beginning to wonder about the role of the superintendent and his close affiliation with the teachers. Is he "their" man, representing their interests and concerns? Or is he helping the teachers to accomplish their ends?

The superintendents claim that they have looked in vain for the models upon which to base a definition of their roles in this new situation. Neither the industrial nor the military models are valid for an organization of highly trained professionals who are capable of making many, if not most, of their own decisions. Where is the locus of authority in a non-paternalistic organization? Where is the link with other social systems? Where is the agency for the protection of the public and the educational opportunities of children? How do you coordinate such a group, and maintain centrality of control while maximizing involvement on all levels? How do you maintain communication and effective effort among all levels of the organization? These are clearly undergirding issues for which good answers are not readily available.

The educational administrator has long felt that his role is one of keeping harmony among the diverse groups with which he works. However, with the new teacher militancy, he can no longer be the helmsman who charts the direction and maintains the organization free from conflict. The teachers' organizations now see conflict as a means for achieving their objectives. The superintendent may now be viewed as a professional adviser for management, from whom they must extract the maximum number of concessions. His freedom of action must be restricted in order to assure teachers a formally recognized voice.

The revolt against paternalism is reflected in other contextual areas as well. The superintendent now finds it difficult to exercise authority over groups in the community which formerly accepted his decisions or those of the board, but who now demand a voice in the making of decisions. Formerly, the superintendent could draw a distinction between matters of public policy and those of professional concern, but community groups now press him for a voice even in the employment, evaluation, and retention of teachers.

Not the least of the superintendent's concerns are those related to his dealing with racial minorities and economically deprived groups who until recently were isolated and alienated from decision-making in the public schools. Today, these groups are well organized. They have aggressive leadership. They are resentful of the years of official discrimination and subordination which they have experienced, and they are clamoring for a voice in shaping those policies which will solve the bitter problems confronting them, reverse the denial of opportunity and provide them their full democratic rights.

The superintendents readily acknowledged that they did not know how to communicate and work with the leaders or with the rank and file of these groups which formerly had made no demands for involvement in the decision-making process. The superintendents indicated that they knew how to deal with the power structure and the middle class groups which control the economic affairs of the community. But these new groups presented challenges to the stability of the school organization and presented problems of communication both by virtue of the fact that they did not accept the traditional authority structure of the school and that they were striving to achieve goals which previously had been outside of the normal aspiration and value structures of the schools. Superintendents fear that these groups are bent upon restricting their freedom of decision-making. These groups refuse to be subordinated to the authority of others even if the decisions made are benevolent because they recognize that such subordination is, in effect, discrimination and denial of their rights.

Superintendents are also experiencing a resurgence of parental interest in and demands upon the schools. They report that there is a change in parental attitudes. Formerly, parents seemed inclined to accept the decisions of educators, to reinforce their discipline in the home, and to seek ways in which they could make adaptations in their living to the requirements of the schools. Now, parents no longer reinforce school officials nor accept their authority to make decisions regarding either their children or educational practices and policies. They question decisions and demand explanations. They exercise their powers to restrict the educators' freedom of action and they demand a voice in the evaluation of the schools and the consideration of new programs and policies before they are inaugurated. Different patterns of public relations are essential, and the superintendent finds he spends much of his time listening to and consulting with a variety of parental groups.

Not only do the adults of the community challenge the authority of educators, but student unrest in the colleges is now spreading to high schools. Many adolescents in our culture feel that they are ready to make mature decisions. Even if they aren't, they seek relief from the constant subordination under which they live by demanding the right to be involved in making the decisions which affect their welfare and determine the boundaries of their conduct. They have studied democratic governance, and they want it applied to the administration of these institutions of which they are a part.

Even in the area of intergovernmental relationships, the role of the specialist in education no longer enjoys the respect it once commanded. The politicians are now making learned pronouncements about educational policy and insisting that educators take due cognizance of their perspectives.

All of these factors indicate that forces within both the school organization and the broader society demand a changing role for the superintendent. He is no longer so much the director of the organization as the mediator between groups. The technologies he needs include not only the determination of the educational consequences of his decisions but also those that enable him to analyze and assess the tolerance for particular kinds of decisions among the various publics of the schools.

The superintendent is becoming much more the individual who is helping to structure the processes through which the decisions are made rather than the one who is formulating the decisions himself. With some feeling, superintendents have asked for aid in determining whether or not current trends are desirable, if not inevitable, and what their proper response to them should be.

Clinging to the traditional views of their roles, the superintendents have varied responses to the challenges to their paternalism. Some view their role as the defender of the traditional values of education against an incipient anarchism. They charge that special interest groups are striving to use the schools as devices for gaining their own political, social, or economic ends. Others make various types of accommodations to the demands of the different groups for direct involvement. None seems to be entirely satisfied that he has found the best answer. Some view the new trends as a challenge for the improvement of education and not as a threat. Whatever their feelings, there is a general recognition of the fact that the schools are caught up in a new social current. If a careful analysis of the situation is not made and the future roles of all involved in the schools' affairs are not charted, the decisions will be made as a result of power plays or rule by expedience.

(2) *Urbanization.* Regardless of where one resides in contemporary American society, his life is affected in many ways by the rapid urbanization which has occurred. Slums and the provision of services for masses of people, significant as they are, are not the only problems which characterize the urban community. The urban society is also characterized by increased job specialization, remoteness of relationships, interdependence among people and functions, heterogeneity of values and goals, diversification and the need for standardization, and, for many individuals, a distinction between the residential and the occupational communities.

Not the least of the difficulties which arise for school administrators in the urban community is that which entails the specialization of relationships. In the rural community, everyone may be involved in multiple behavioral settings with almost everyone else. The superintendent may not only see his board members at official meetings of the school board, but he may belong to a lodge or a service club with them. He may play golf with them. Some of them will belong to the same church, and some of them may be working together on particular community committees. There is almost constant face-to-face contact among individuals involved in the same types of activities, with the same kinds of benefits and responsibilities. The sense of community is more readily established, and the stake which individuals have in the community is relatively the same as that of their neighbors.

In the urbanized community, few of these relationships are possible. The school board member, whether he be in the suburban community or the central city, is very likely to work in a community different from the one in which he resides and where his children go to school. His only contact with the superintendent of schools may be in connection with his official role and responsibilities. In fact, relatively few people with whom the superintendent deals will have any relationship with him in any other role than that as the superintendent of schools.

The fact that the basic techniques, perspectives, and processes of school administration were established for an agrarian rather than an urbanized society presents problems to the superintendent. As some superintendents recognized, the preparatory programs for school administrators are still oriented toward the smaller community where the superintendent is a very visible figure both to his staff and to the majority of the citizens.

Now the superintendent has to deal with new problems that arise from the size of the school organization, the remoteness of relationships, and the widening boundaries of the community. The school staff can no longer be "one big happy family," working toward the same objectives. Bureaucratic processes must be developed to maintain and operate the organization. Standardized forms and procedures for communication among different levels of the organization have to be employed. Decisions have to become standardized and based upon definitely stated policies in order to maintain equity, avoid favoritism, and reduce the possibility of idiosyncratic decisions on the part of subordinate administrators.

The school today is also thrown into relationships with other governmental agencies which are concerned with the problems of youth and, in the broader sense, must be considered educational institutions. Their policies might differ from those of the school, and their powers of independent decision-making may create difficult problems of coordination among youth-serving agencies. The school is in competition with these agencies, both for the support of the citizens and for the tax dollars that are needed for their maintenance. The officials with whom the superintendent deals are not necessarily his neighbors or parents of his students. They have their own political objectives and their attitude toward the schools may be determined by the degree to which the school assists or impairs the achievement of these political goals.

The community problems with which the administrator has to deal become almost overwhelming, both in their sheer magnitude and in the expenditures necessary to solve them. The superintendent's freedom of action to make educational solutions to problems is greatly restricted.

It is restricted, first, by the fact that he has to take into consideration the perspectives of so many groups. If he wishes to survive he has to develop refined skills for working with a large number of groups and for achieving some balance among the various demands and objectives which they offer.

He is restricted by the organizational layers through which his communications must pass. He no longer can have direct contact with many teachers. He depends upon intermediaries to provide him information about what is happening in the school, and he relies on the same intermediaries to communicate his directives throughout the school organization. He must also deal with large segments of the public through his agents, but he recognizes that intermediaries either naturally or intentionally distort communications. As a consequence, he is never certain that what is reported to him is correct nor that which is reported *from* him bears the message that he intended.

He is restricted by the willingness and the readiness of the staff, who are remote from him, to pursue the same educational goals and to facilitate the plans and programs the board adopts. The literature tells him and the school board that it is the leadership of the superintendent that is vital to effecting change and improvement within the school organization; but to effect change or to modify practices, the superintendent will have to work through other subordinate administrators in the central office, supervisors and coordinators, principals and teachers, as well as the PTA presidents, and the representatives of various local pressure and special interest groups.

The superintendent is restricted by the tremendous costs that might be required to make even minor modifications. Simple changes in pupil-teacher ratios may cause as much as a ten percent increase in the instructional budget. And each proposal for change has to be weighed against the variety of normal, competing pressures for the utilization of funds.

While beset with the internal problems of the urbanized school system, the superintendent is also forced to acknowledge that the school can play a very important role in attempting to resolve the difficult social problems that exist within the urbanized community. Problems of crime, delinquency, economic disadvantage, and racial discrimination are all magnified in the densely populated community. When a large percentage of pupils engage in gang warfare, the superintendent of schools cannot maintain that this is solely the concern of other officials within the community. Violence is as likely to break out at a basketball game, during the lunch hour, or in the corridors while students are passing between classes as on the central street of the worst slums in the community. There may be a strong compulsion on the part of educators to insist that the schools must be concerned exclusively with instruction, but realism dictates that it must be equally concerned with the conditions of community life which affect the ability of students to participate in and profit from the programs offered by the schools.

The urbanized community is governmentally defined within certain geographical boundaries, but the problems of the school district, as well as of other governmental units, can be neither confined within those boundaries nor resolved exclusively within them. Racial imbalance within the city, in many instances, cannot be solved while its suburban satellites remain all white, real estate costs and restrictions (even if "extra-legal") prevent the entry of racial minorities, and attendance boundaries remain rigid either through practice or policy. The institutional forms for solving problems among a variety of governmental jurisdictions have rarely been established, and there is provincialism and jealousy among patrons and officials to guard their favored positions and to prevent the suburb's becoming "lost" as just another sub-division of the city.

Faced with these problems and their many ramifications, the superintendent can realistically question his professional preparation. The theory of organization (if it may be dignified as such) which dominates in educational administration was formulated before many schools were faced with these kinds of problems. There is no technology of school administration worked out for the bureaucratic school organization. There are no fundamental principles available to be used as guides for determining the point at which the size of school units restricts the adequacy of educational effectiveness. There is no good theory established to guide the superintendent in determining at what point he needs additional administrative subordinates, supervisors, and coordinators to assist in carrying on the business of the schools. There are few guidelines which can realistically be used in determining the points and conditions under which the school organization has to be decentralized. Certainly, since Counts wrote *Dare the School Build a New Social Order?* the educational profession has either been involved in aimless controversy relative to the role of the school with respect to critical social issues or it has adopted an ostrich-like position when confronted with them. The school no longer exists as an independent agency of the urbanized community, but the principles of administration which the superintendent studied in college still claim that it does.

(3) *The Persistence of the Ethos of Jeffersonian Agrarianism.* In spite of our rapid urbanization and industrialization, much of our social philosophy is still based upon the concept of a simple, agrarian democracy, characterized by a faith in the ability of the people on the grass roots level to solve their own problems in their own, independent way. Throughout the history of this nation, there arose a fierce independence of spirit, a desire to maintain decision-making authority "at the grass roots levels," a distrust of centralization, and a fear of federal control. A system of checks and balances permeated all forms of corporate life so that one branch of government maintained a check against each other level of government.

In no arena was the concept of local control, arising out of a Jeffersonian agrarianism, more predominant than in the field of education. The local control of education became one of those grand principles, draped in sanctity and hallowed as a foundation stone upon which the persistence of this nation depended. It is a rallying cry even though the record of its accomplishments for education is very inconsistent.

It must be acknowledged that through the local control of education a strong educational system was built in the United States, but it did not develop as a mechanism which is adaptive to the changing needs of society. For every one of its accomplishments, there was a counterpart of failure. Extensive vocational educational programs were not developed until the federal government in cooperation with the states provided funds through which programs could be inaugurated in the schools. The local schools did not assume the responsibility for the education of atypical children until funds were forthcoming from both the state and the federal government to support programs through stimulative grants. Neither Northern nor Southern school districts endeavored to relieve the educational disadvantages caused by segregation of the races until after the Supreme Court's decision of 1954 and the multitude of court decisions which resulted from the resistance of local school districts in all parts of the country to fulfill their national obligations. The special problems of dropouts, particularly of economically disadvantaged children, have been with the schools for decades, but it is only within the last few years, under subventions of the federal government, that approaches to the solutions of these problems have been formulated.

In spite of the record, there is considerable criticism of federal aid programs and the amount of federal restriction that accompanies categorical aid for specific programs. Superintendents are accustomed to working within the framework of the local school district where sentiments for local control run high. To represent their school boards and their communities adequately, they must adopt attitudes of criticism or defensiveness when confronted with these federal programs. The two strong constraints upon the superintendent—his preparatory program and his socialization as an administrator—both tend to force him to accept the concept of local control as the viable principle upon which school organization is established. No rationale has been fully developed for his working within the limitations imposed by a sharing of decision-making powers with the federal and state governments.

In spite of popular sentiments, there is a recognition by superintendents that the improvement of education is dependent upon the establishment of adequate working relations among the various levels of government. They recognize that the taxing power of the federal government is more efficient and more inclusive than that of any other agency, and if new money is to come to education to enable it to solve some of its problems, almost inevitably it has to come from the federal government. They also recognize that the expansion of the educational program into neglected areas or where resources have not been adequate to the tasks imposed can now be accomplished on a broad scale only through federal intervention. To the extent that it is within the national interest for new programs to be developed, the federal government cannot rely upon its powers of persuasion over local power structures to provide resources to the necessary ends. Local school districts have not allocated sufficient funds for the relief of the economically underprivileged or the stimulation of changed curriculum patterns which are necessary for the training of manpower to meet our national needs.

The philosophy of inter-governmental relations in education has been dominated by the agrarianism of the rural community. There is much evidence to suggest that USOE was long dominated by state superintendents coming from the more agrarian states, and state legislatures, in turn, have kept state departments of education weak and ineffective in the performance of their educational responsibilities because they did not want strong state departments of education which could impose standards or other controls upon local school districts.

Many of the superintendents recognized that local autonomy has meant the right of the local district to be irresponsible with respect to its educational programs. Criteria of economy have sometimes dominated decision-making. In some places the narrow educational views of influential dominants have caused boards and superintendents to restrict the full development of programs to meet the educational needs of the total community. Although superintendents and their boards cling to the concept of local control, many superintendents recognized that local irresponsibility or indifference toward the expansion of education into neglected areas is a luxury which society can no longer afford.

Superintendents recognize that federal programs must persist and that certain controls must be established, but the rationale for the acceptance of money and controls in the light of the philosophy of local control has produced a near schizoid condition for many superintendents. Many have taken an opportunistic stance, justifying acceptance only on the basis that local money is involved and will be paid to the federal government in taxes whether or not the local district takes advantage of the funds. Many have felt that after acceptance they had to demonstrate to their boards and communities some resistance to federal regulations in order to justify their protection of the independent decision-making powers of the local school district. Many have had to defend the federal programs against a whole new group of school critics who are opposed to all federal subventions and the local school district's becoming a "partner to the crime" by participating in federally financed programs. In conforming to highly emotionalized community pressures, some superintendents publicly criticized particular federal guidelines even though they privately admitted that they are essential to implement Congressional objectives for establishing programs and that definite educational benefits have accrued from them.

The superintendent is in a precarious position on issues involving state and federal relations. He is responsible for procuring the resources needed to develop adequate educational programs. He is the man in the middle between groups which hold disparate views on the function of education in helping to solve the critical problems of youth in our society. Yet, he is basically without the professional guidelines he needs to aid him in this conflict. There is no generally accepted or well-established rationale for his role among the inter-relationships of various governmental units and their responsibilities toward education. Whom does he represent? The community and board who employ him? Or some idealized responsibility toward "education" and the educational goals of the broader society? No one in educational administration has given him the security of a defensible position upon which he can stand.

In no way does a society in transition produce greater tension and potential for conflict than in the disparity that arises between traditionally sanctioned attitudes and the behaviors that are essential in the light of modern conditions. In the United States today, the traditional attitudes toward local control are no longer adequate guides to action. If the superintendent wishes to survive in his community, he cannot be the leader in developing a new perspective or rationale of the inter-relationships of various governmental levels. However, his work will be seriously impeded until that rationale becomes established.

(4) *Cultural Pluralism and the Decline of the Dominance of the "Protestant Ethic."*[2] Although the ideal of American education is the

---

[2] As we use the term "Protestant Ethic," herein, it refers to a set of social values as identified by Max Weber in his classic *The Protestant Ethic and the Spirit of Capitalism.* According to Weber, the social values undergirding Protestantism led to the rise of modern capitalism. These values, regardless of the religious beliefs to which individuals subscribed, became the basis for middle-class values in American

effective education of all of the children of all of the people, it is apparent that the ideal is far from realized. The present program of federal inter- ventions is but a modest attempt to rectify the inequities that have been accumulating for several decades. To a considerable extent, the emer- gence of the universal education system in the United States was a re- sponse to the challenges of immigration. The major thrust of the public schools was the socialization of immigrant children to the American way of life and, particularly, to those values and aspirations that are congruent with the so-called "Protestant ethic" and, presumably, the foundation upon which a capitalistic society is established. In the process of the socialization of the immigrant and his children, the effort was made to build a homogeneous society based upon a prescribed set of values.

The focus of attention was upon the socialization of the western Euro- pean immigrant. The indigenous minority and the non-European immi- grants who were readily identified by the color of their skin and by their cultural differences were neglected through indifference, economic exploitation, or plain bigotry.

The large number of children who formed the new generation of the rapidly expanding urban proletariat, many of whom were of racial mi- nority groups, were similarly slighted by the public schools. Coming from economically disadvantaged homes, these children could not readily comprehend or internalize the aspirations of the officially prescribed middle-class values of the public schools. As a consequence, the prevalent

---

society. In the United States, during the latter part of the 19th century, they became all but institutionalized as the "official American values" through the rise and domi- nance of social Darwinism. They, accordingly, became the dominant value structure of the American schools. Tempering Weber's formulation somewhat, Albert K. Cohen lists nine beliefs as a part of this system of values: (1) Ambition is a virtue, while its absence is a defect or sign of maladjustment; (2) resourcefulness and self-reliance are applauded, and the individual is encouraged to stand on his own and not turn to others for help; (3) high valuation is placed on the cultivation of skills and on the tangible achievements which presumably result from both skill and effort; (4) also highly valued is "worldly asceticism," a readiness and ability to postpone and sub- ordinate immediate satisfactions and self-indulgence in the interests of achieving long-run goals (industry and thrift are desirable ends in themselves); (5) rationality, economical living, budgeting, careful planning—all are prized; (6) the cultivation of good manners, courtesy, and pleasing personality is encouraged; (7) physical aggres- sion should be controlled, any form of violence is taboo, and one should have as good relations as possible with other people; (8) all time should be spent in worthwhile activities, and even recreation should be "wholesome"; (9) property should be re- spected and prized. See, Albert K. Cohen, *Delinquent Boys: The Culture of the Gang.* (Glencoe: Free Press, 1955), pp. 84-93. See also, Max Weber, *The Protestant Ethic and the Spirit of Capitalism.* (New York: Scribners, 1958). Richard Hofstadter, *Social Darwinism in American Thought.* (Boston: The Beacon Press, 1955).

social Darwinism of the nineteenth and early twentieth centuries ascribed to them an inferior status. The typically middle-class teacher and administrator had difficulty in understanding these children or in accommodating educational content and methods to their special needs.

Accompanying the increasing urbanization of our society was an extensive fragmentation and dispersion of the value systems of American society. To educate all of the children of all of the people, the schools still must find the means to adapt themselves to the varying levels of aspirations and values of the different groups which comprise American society.

The social pathologies of the latter half of the twentieth century have become so intense that society can no longer afford to neglect these groups nor completely isolate them from the good and desirable things which society has to offer. Politicians have come to recognize that these groups constitute potentially powerful blocks of voters. To maintain political power a party has to take into consideration their value orientations, their needs and aspirations, and distribute to them some of the goods which are now enjoyed by the more fortunate classes.

The predominant school policy toward many of these children has been to expect behavioral conformance on the same level that could be expected of the children who come from middle-class homes. Failure to comply has meant that they are either officially thrown out of school or subjected to such negative sanctions that they are psychologically "locked out" of school.

The official policies and subventions of the federal government today make it imperative that the school adapt its program to the needs of these youngsters. At the same time the leadership of many groups has come to recognize the political power which they possess. They are no longer docile, conforming groups eagerly awaiting and thankful for the scarce hand-outs which may be given to them. They are not content with the schools' *pro forma* compliance. They not only demand full compliance, but they also demand full involvement in the making of policies and the formulating of solutions.

As previously indicated, superintendents have tended to feel comfortable in their relationships with dominant power structures of the community. One cannot criticize them on this account, since these are the people on school boards to whom superintendents have been responsible. The value patterns of superintendents, we suspect, have been shaped by their reliance upon and their close associations with these groups within the community. The economic level of the superintendents is, of course, more on a par with that of the "economic influentials" than with that of those subordinate groups with whom they are now coming into contact and with whose problems they must increasingly become concerned.

There has been a crippling deficiency of research on the problems of diverse value structures in relation to the values generally prescribed by the schools and upheld both by educators and those charged with the governance of the schools. Schools exist to prepare individuals for their future or adult roles in society, and, in this sense, are an official instrument for the maintenance of the future-oriented middle-class values. Educators who place great stress upon these values are subject to the favorable sanctions of those who govern and administer the schools. Typically, students and parents who cannot comprehend or are unwilling to conform to these standards have been considered as educationally pathological. There is increasing evidence, however, that the future-oriented school has great difficulty adjusting its program to serve groups within the community whose futures are bleak and who are stretched to the limits of their resources and energy merely for immediate survival.

The great problem facing school administrators in this situation is that of how to make the school relevant for these groups; how to so structure the school program that it is rich and meaningful for these children within the context and values of their lives and aspirations; how, in other words, to help them understand that the school is an instrument through which they can achieve a desirable future life. The essential issue for the educator is that for these children who are, everywhere, bombarded with middle-class values and aspirations, while denied the means for achieving them, the schools must become an instrument which gives them a future.

Unfortunately, the implications of these needs have not been worked out in detail for the schools nor for the operating patterns of superintendents and subordinate administrators. Alert superintendents realize that they have great difficulty in communicating satisfactorily with the leaders of minority and disadvantaged groups, and they also perceive that principals and teachers have difficulty understanding and communicating with the children and parents of these groups. There is a general feeling that preparatory institutions have not helped future teachers understand the cultural differences which exist among sub-cultures of American society, nor have they developed the adjustments and accommodations necessary to make the schools a vital part of growing up for *all* children. To find these adjustments for the schools is a matter of prime importance today.

(5) *Search for Identity and Guiding Values.* Associated with all these factors is the current search for a sense of identification within the community and a set of guiding values upon which behavior can be based and through which the individual can achieve his goals. The subjugation of the individual to the mass, the breakdown of traditional patterns of behavior, the persistence of traditional institutions and social processes, the growing heterogeneity of the value systems of the community as a concommitant of urbanization—all are factors in the alienation of individuals.

Undoubtedly, educators, too, frequently have feelings of alienation in the urbanized community. On numerous occasions, superintendents recalled nostalgically the happy situation that prevailed when they were teachers and administrators in relatively small, rural schools. There they could look upon the staff as a happy family in a community which was more ready to accept them and accord them prestige appropriate to the status which they held in society. Their memory is probably idealized and painted with somewhat brighter colors than it deserves to be, but it indicates that the sense of belonging to a definite community and being a part of discrete groups which could live amicably and purposefully together, in retrospect, gives them a sense of well-being which they lack amidst the frustrations and conflicts of their present positions.

The school is caught in a thick web of conflicting demands. The search for identity without clearly established goals leads to confusion. The failure of individuals to put their requests and demands into perspectives in relation to possible alternatives leads to greater insistence that their demands be met without compromise. As the superintendents frequently mentioned, parents seem to compensate for frustration and confusion by reverting to an almost infantile aggressiveness when dealing with public agencies which control programs affecting their children. Apparently as a result of the frustrations that arise from the failure to belong in contemporary society, the political and social behaviors of individuals become caricatures of their true personalities, but school officials and teachers have to work with individuals as they reveal themselves. The schools have officially and professionally designated responsibilities toward all children regardless of the conflicts they experience through their homes.

In some agrarian societies, children were prized because of their ability to produce goods for the family. In many segments of our society children are prized because of the prestige that they may be able to bring to their families through their educational accomplishments and in compensation for the failure of their parents to achieve a satisfying status on their own. In this situation, the school is very much a part of the child's problem. The traditional values which it attempts to reinforce may be in conflict with the values and perspectives acquired by the children in their homes. The values and behaviors legitimated in the school may be ridiculed in the home, and *vice versa*. The school may also be in conflict with the parental aspirations for the child when it recognizes that parental aspirations are unrealistic and do not take into consideration the child's limitations. The defense of the parent, seemingly, is to become further alienated from an official body of society, critical of the schools, and a ready prey of extremist groups which seek to subvert the broader functions of public education.

The docile and the accepting, the satisfied and the self-sufficient, produce few problems for the superintendent and absorb but little, if any, of his time. However, out of dissatisfaction, frustration, tension, and despair arises either apathy or aggressive behavior which threatens the superintendent, as well as other school personnel, and which also mobilizes those of like mind into movements which, in the minds of superintendents, produce instability within the schools. For these latter groups, the school may not be a haven or refuge. For them it may be a hostile institution, fostered by a society with growing laxity of standards and dangerous proclivities, to which they are forced to send their children in spite of their own inclinations and in defiance of the values which they accept. There can be no question that for the school administrator the presence of the antagonisms so easily aroused is a major disruptive force.

It is apparent that changes are needed in the public schools, but the superintendent is wont to ask, "What directions shall the changes take? Who shall determine the directions for the future of the public schools? How flexible can the schools become? What interest groups need to be heard? How do educators sift legitimate criticism from those that are politically inspired and designed to help some special interest group gain power?" He might also ask at what point he can expect other governmental and educational agencies to take some of the burden off his shoulders.

(6) *Technology*. The schools are not immune from the problems imposed by the advances of modern, scientific technology. It is now possible to perform by machine almost any labor performed by human beings. It is also possible to extend the range of the human mind far beyond the limitations which human physiology imposes upon it.

Many of the superintendents, as well as those who study administration, must wonder if the computer is making the current superintendent obsolete in his job. There can be no question that machines have the potential to greatly alter the job of the administrator. Many tasks which the administrator formerly performed inefficiently by hand can be done more rapidly, more effectively, and more thoroughly by machine, for example, scheduling of classes and routines. Machine processes applied to business practices expedite operations, but also necessitate a greater degree of centralization than was true of hand operations. Most significant, to the administrator, if he finds the means for using the technology, is the manner in which machines can handle information and supply him and the school board not only with data which are needed to make decisions, but also with an analysis of the relationships of variables having a bearing upon the outcomes of the decision process. Techniques such as systems analysis, program budgeting, Program Evaluation and Review Technique (PERT), and manpower assessment are in emergent stages as applied to educational administration. They extend the ability of the administrator to evaluate the effectiveness of the organization, to relate cost and resource inputs to achievement outputs, to identify resources needed to obtain specific goals, to plan for the adaptability of the organization to meet emergent needs, and to make decisions more realistically in relation to actual operations and both societal, and organizational requirements. The educational administrator will find it increasingly necessary to understand how to use the knowledge he can acquire from these techniques to coordinate, plan, and evaluate the operations of the schools. It is doubtful if the superintendent must acquire all of the technical knowledge essential for the use of these techniques. However, knowledge of how to apply the information gained from these devices is essential for the superintendent. Preparatory programs for administrators must include studies of these techniques, and in-service education programs are needed for those now engaged in the superintendency.

Not the least of the problems arising from the applications of modern technology to educational administration is that of defining new roles in the administrative structure of the schools. When it had but little information about its operations, the school system could comfortably exist without a central information and research agency, and only the largest school districts in the country had such services. School administrators can no longer operate justifiably without such a service. In most school districts it was formerly possible to argue that the continuous evaluation of school operations, both service and instructional, was not possible for lack of instrumentalities through which data collected could be economically analyzed. Such claims are no longer valid. Research, development, evaluation, coordination—all are now the central functions of the administrative office, and new roles have to be adapted to accommodate the existing potentials. Machines will not make decisions, but they are invaluable in the decision-making of a complex organization. Machines are not self-generated; they have to be programmed to do the jobs which administrators want done. Positions have to be established within the administrative team which are staffed by people with knowledge of the potentials of machine operations and how they can be applied to the operations of the organization. How to use this new technology effectively is a challenge to all administrators.

Superintendents are aware that many of the jobs for which children now in school must be trained have not as yet been completely identified. And yet, without this identification, the school must at least provide the foundations for their entry into these occupations. At the same time that the school is preparing children for the future, the superintendent must wonder what he is going to do with the human and the physical resources which the district has acquired at great cost but which are suitable only for preparing children to live in the past. The implications of the technological revolution necessitate a re-evaluation of every phase of school operations, but where can the superintendent, if he has a mind to, find the trained personnel who themselves have not become obsolescent and can make an objective and disinterested appraisal of present school programs in relationship to future social needs?

Determining how to phase in new programs (and obtain qualified people to operate them) and phase out old programs (and still find room in the organization for those individuals who maintained them and seemingly cannot be retooled for the newer programs), imposes difficult burdens upon the superintendent and changes his relationships with personnel throughout the organization. Many are concerned lest the dehumanization of work processes result equally in the inhuman treatment of individuals who used their skills effectively when their skills were still pertinent.

Technology builds products to sell, and these do not come cheap. A completely modern classroom using all of the contemporary technology related to instruction that can reasonably be employed would be several times more expensive to construct than the traditional four walls with a few windows and some desks, chairs, chalkboards, and book shelves.

When the superintendent finds the community increasingly reluctant to provide the bare four walls for its children, how can resources be obtained to up-date its instructional technology with the expensive new gadgetry?

Possibly even more expensive than the gadgetry itself is the human cost of implementing it. Human beings must be refurbished, but these human beings are not youngsters; they are mature men and women who have heavy commitments for the welfare of others. If society no longer has use for their skills but needs them to operate within the framework of a new technology, who must bear the expense for their maintenance and retraining? The retraining and renewal of the superintendent himself poses a financial burden upon society. Not all of the expense, certainly, can be borne by the individual.

A further concern relates to the evaluation of the host of technological devices that are on the market, all purporting to be better than those of their competitors. Madison Avenue learned of the power of justifying a product on the basis of research which indicates its effectiveness long before the federal government, colleges and universities, and the public schools. In some instances, it has not been too difficult to buy researchers to work in the best economic interests of their employers. How do superintendents with the limited resources and skills at their command evaluate all of these claims in order to maximize the utilization of the district's scarce dollars for educational advantages? Superintendents feel that they need the assistance of agencies outside of the schools to evaluate claims made for products, but the comparative evaluations are fraught with both public relations and legal implications. Even more than just product evaluation, the problems of finding the best educational uses of technology within the fabric of the educational enterprise pose a severe challenge to the schools and suggest an extension of the teacher's role beyond the requirements of the classroom. All of these considerations involve expenditures beyond traditional limits.

These questions are new and it is difficult to find valid answers to them. Educators fear that the answers are coming from sources with an economic stake in the products. They feel that sufficient effort is not coming from the public domain to help them find those solutions which will guarantee an effective use of modern technology for the educational program. Neither administrative nor instructional operations can afford to ignore the technological advances which give promise of helping the schools achieve greater quality of teaching and more effective management. But planning and evaluation outside of normal operations are necessary, and many superintendents fear that the resources needed will not be provided by local districts.

In Summary

One cannot view these data without recognizing that it is not humanly possible for the superintendents to spend their time in the management and direction of the school districts, working with the many individuals and groups that now comprise the publics of the public schools, and still find time for the contemplation and study necessary to devise master strategies for overcoming the barriers created by these problems and for developing the technologies needed to deal effectively with the problems confronting the schools.

The natural inclination of other agencies when confronted with these problems is to suggest, "Let's do some research!" More research is obviously needed. The improvement of the knowledge relative to the milieu in which school administrators operate is essential. A better understanding of the phenomena with which the school administrator deals and the variables which can change the consequences of administrative interventions is imperative, but the production of knowledge by itself is no guarantee that it will be used. As Robert Lynd[3] discovered in his provocative study entitled, *Knowledge for What?* in 1939, the problem is not so much that of accumulating more knowledge as finding means for the effective utilization of that which we have.

One of our difficulties is that we rely so heavily upon scientific investigation that we tend to discourage other means for the validation of understanding. Some years ago the sociologist, Alfred McClung Lee, suggested that there should be a concern for the training of practical men of affairs as "clinical students of society."[4] In his conception, two results could be achieved if these men could find a means for communicating among themselves their observations, techniques, and insights, much the same as psychologists and physicians operate within the clinical setting. First, this interaction would help them to refine their ability to diagnose the situations which confront them and test the validity of remedies to the pathologies they discover. Second, through the utilization of the knowledge, experience, and observations gained from their involvement in practical affairs, they could add vastly to the knowledge storehouse avail-

---

[3] Robert S. Lynd. *Knowledge for What?* (Princeton: Princeton University Press, 1939).

[4] Alfred McClung Lee. "The Clinical Study of Society." *American Sociological Review*, 20:6 (December, 1955) pp. 648-653.

able to the theoreticians and the scientific researchers among the behavioral sciences.

The superintendent has to depend upon his "clinical" insights in dealing with the many problems which confront him. He cannot escape responsibility for decision by calling upon the researcher to provide him with "solutions." The researcher may help the superintendent understand the variables which should be taken into consideration in the formulation of solutions, but the solutions must be found independent of the knowledge about the phenomena which occasioned the problems. The superintendent needs more than knowledge. He needs skills in diagnosing situations, of testing the reactions of relevant groups to his problems, of perceiving the impact of decisions upon various groups, of understanding group values and their relations to his proposals. He must know what is "obtainable" along with what is desirable. Simon draws the useful distinction between economic man who *maximizes* and administrative man who *satisfices*. He compares this to finding the sharpest needle in the haystack as distinct from finding any needle that can do the job. No superintendent exists today without having experience as a mediator and a compromiser.

Politically, the superintendent must work with groups. Even if he could find ideal solutions, the diversities among the groups which are relevant to educational decision-making would force compromises upon him. The superintendent's role is that of finding the strategies through which decisions can be made while minimizing the friction which results. As a "clinical student of society," he should learn to detect the point of friction in the interactions of groups and to diagnose both the functional and the pathological characteristics of situations. Then, he can apply his knowledge and intuitive familiarity to the prescription of remedies. He needs assistance and resources from other groups and agencies, but if the superintendency is to persist in the modern school organization, we suspect he will be more the diagnostician and facilitator than has been true in the past.

8/

Priorities
for
Action

As we sift the data and our own conclusions derived from them, it is apparent that priorities can be viewed from different perspectives. Various agencies have different levels of programs, and each agency appears to be desirous of extending its own operations and realm of effectiveness. What might be a priority from the point of view of the officials of USOE might not be such from the perspective of the state commissioner of education. It might also not be such from the perspective of the college professor or the superintendent of schools. All of them represent segments of the educational profession. None of them can say that he truly represents the point of view that fully reflects the entire educational spectrum. Perhaps one of the most hopeful opportunities for the regional educational laboratories would be to establish constructive working relationships among the various levels of the educational hierarchy. Through the dialogue thus developed, the agencies could use their diverse professional skills in cooperation rather than in competition as now seems the case.

We do not claim to draw from these data the conclusions and recommendations applicable for all individuals and for all agencies. We suggest a series of points for consideration with a full recognition and warning to our readers that these are formulated from a prismatic perception of the data adjusted through our own biases, values, and subjective evaluations. These considerations are presented without reference to their rank, and we believe all of them are worthy of consideration by various agencies.

(1) *Pre-service Preparatory Programs.* The superintendents participating in this study ranged in age from the middle thirties to the middle sixties. Some of them were several generations away from their basic professional, administrative preparation, while others had just emerged from it. Yet, to a man, they felt that both their preparatory programs and the in-service educational opportunities which they have had since entry into administrative posts were far from adequate for preparing them to resolve the problems which daily confront them. In consideration of their reactions and our own cursory examination of some of the major preparatory programs in the country, we suggest as a matter for primary consideration that *preparatory programs for superintendents need to be carefully evaluated and systematically revised.*

On the basis of Katz's[1] three level analysis of the tasks of administrators (the technical, the human, and the conceptual), our analysis shows that preparatory programs tend either to emphasize one area to the exclusion of the others or to present a smattering of experiences in all areas without careful analysis of what goals are being served.

Questions might well be raised as to whether or not the courses that have been traditionally devised to serve the technical needs are truly dealing with the most up-to-date and appropriate technologies. Some appear to be preparing superintendents for administrative roles and tasks which were appropriate in a by-gone age but are no longer the critical concerns of administrators today.

We might also raise the question as to whether the human relations courses present an excessive emphasis upon the academic and disciplinary aspects of human relations without an appropriate emphasis upon building the skills in human relations so vitally needed by administrators on the job.

Conceptual areas, too, may emphasize abstract theory with little or no relevance to the conceptual needs of the superintendent in his daily responsibilities. Professors frequently told us that the students in their classes were smart enough to draw the implications for practice from the theory itself, but superintendents reported that some of their problems arose from a poor conceptual base which they found difficult, if not impossible, to translate to their immediate problems.

One cannot help but wonder if the job of the superintendent today and the problems he confronts have been carefully analyzed and systematically studied to enable professors to devise the most meaningful in-

---

[1] Robert L. Katz. "Skills of an Effective Administrator." *Harvard Business Review*, 33:1 (Jan.-Feb. 1955), pp. 33-42.

structional programs. In only a few universities did it appear to these researchers that institutional funds and professorial time were being allocated to the careful study of these problems and the revision of preparatory programs in accordance with their findings.

Notable in efforts to bring consistency, knowledge, and reason to bear upon the preparatory problems of educational administrators is the program of the University Council for Educational Administration. For the most part its publications on the topics are sound, and its explorations present numerous worthy approaches to the resolution of inadequacies. With limited resources, UCEA has won a deservedly high reputation. When pressed to respond to how these publications were being used, representatives of colleges and universities, for the most part, could indicate no systematic employment of these new conceptual tools relative to preparatory programs within their own institution and applied to their own programs. They might affect the activities of individual professors, but there are few instances, seemingly, of how they have resulted in major modifications of programs. One reason for this state of affairs may be that recommendations are almost entirely subjective and not adequately supported by basic research. *The Federal government could render invaluable assistance through its support of basic research and developmental projects in professional preparation programs.*

There appears to be a dangerous proliferation of administrative preparatory programs in most states. Every institution regardless of the breadth of its graduate resources seemingly wants to become involved in administrative preparatory programs. Most of these programs, despite the size of their enrollments, do not meet the standards of the NCATE nor the criteria for admission into UCEA. Yet, students are being prepared for their professional vocations, and precious resources of the states are being allocated to these programs. Since most of the preparatory programs for the superintendency now involve work beyond the Master's Degree, as required for membership by the AASA, it is questionable that adequate preparatory programs can be mounted in universities without fully established graduate programs through the doctorate. Since it is recognized that much of the knowledge base which the administrator needs is offered in disciplines outside of the schools of education, it is doubtful that an adequate administrative preparatory program can be established in any institution which does not have doctoral programs in all of the fields of the behavioral sciences and in several of the fields of the humanities. These criteria are suggested without refutation in the studies made by UCEA and the criteria determined after deliberation by

NCATE, but these factors have not deterred the expansion of programs and institutions without adequate resources from using their political influence to gain entry to the field.

Before administrators can be effective, they must have adequate preparation for their positions. Administration today, as numerous studies show, involves the application of knowledge and the employment of skills. But both the knowledge base and the technology change, and administrators can readily become obsolescent. A key to the retardation of obsolescence is the degree to which preparatory programs forecast and project developments within both the field and society and become oriented both to the present and future rather than remain static and traditional in their approach. Few institutions today are engaged in forecasting the future needs of the field and adjusting their programs accordingly.

One of the serious obstacles to adequate preparatory programs is the lack of sufficient standards for staffing university positions in educational administration. If the charges of the superintendents are true—and they are certainly worthy of investigation—many of the programs are staffed with individuals who cannot relate effectively to the administrator in the larger school districts today nor deal adequately in their preparatory courses with the problems which these administrators confront.

Not only developing adequate standards of staffing but utilizing appropriately the time of professors of educational administration is a matter for serious concern. With the increasing numbers of students entering higher education, with increased patronage of graduate programs, and with demands for the internal utilization within universities of the time, experience, and skill of those who have administrative ability, it appears that many professors of educational administration are overburdened with work, spend much of their time outside of their teaching responsibilities on administrative chores, and are not given the time for careful consideration of the problems with which they must deal.

Although these factors vary from university to university, the diversity of attention paid to such details indicates that universities are not allocating the necessary resources to the preparation of educational administration. Unitl they recognize the importance of this field, the quality of the public schools is likely to suffer.

In all of the major professions, preparatory programs are accredited upon the basis of professional standards of preparation to insure that programs contain the range of content and skill-building experiences necessary for competent practices in the field, that teachers in the programs are fully qualified for their responsibilities in the preparation programs, and that universities allocate sufficient resources to maintain the quality of the program. Standards have been developed by NCATE, but they are applied only to institutions when they ask for accreditation. Most states do not require NCATE approval for accreditation of certification programs. UCEA has carefully devised standards for membership, but they are applied exclusively to universities which ask for membership. It has no continuing evaluation after membership is granted. The AASA has standards for membership, but programs leading to qualification for membership do not have to be approved by NCATE. Many institutions of higher education have resisted accreditation procedures because these procedures seemingly restrict local control and freeze standards. Accreditation standards, however, exist to protect the public against the entry of unqualified practitioners into the field. Without them, substandard programs are permitted to flourish. *States should require that no less than NCATE standards prevail among institutions which prepare administrators for certification.* If NCATE standards are not adequate or appropriate, they should be reviewed and revised, but until this can be demonstrated, they constitute an important vehicle for maintaining minimum levels of professional preparation which are essential for the provision of qualified educational administrators.

(2) *In-service Educational Programs.* Professionals faced with the tensions of their jobs and constant engagement in critical problems can rapidly become professionally obsolescent unless many opportunities for self-renewal are both available to them and demanded of them. A review of the in-service educational opportunities available to superintendents throughout the country presents a very discouraging picture. Few, if any, of the programs are based upon a realistic perception of the needs of administrators in the field. Few appear to be established upon sound principles of professional education. Few seem to be developed with any consistency of effort toward the attainment of well established goals, and relatively few receive from school superintendents the patronage which they want.

Noticeably lacking in the federal programs for upgrading the educational profession are specific programs designed for either principals or superintendents. Noticeably lacking in the professional requirements of the AASA are criteria for their members' engaging in in-service education to maintain currency of knowledge and skills. Noticeably lacking in the budgets of schools of education is provision for the expenditure of funds for the in-service education of administrators in the field.

The typical program involving three days of listening to speakers and engaging in "bull sessions," is hardly an adequate device for the in-service education of administrators today. We would agree with Professor Lee that the "practical man of affairs" in charge of the public schools should be a clinical student of society and that one of his foremost needs is the constant testing of his ability to perceive the factors which are relevant to his decision-making, to analyze the consequences of different types of interventions, and to improve his ability to deal with these situations through a careful evaluation of the experiences of his peers. He must also have opportunities to study the current research and developments in his field under guidance of individuals qualified to help him draw the implications for his practice and the refinement of his skills.

To operate successful in-service education programs for administrators, sponsoring agencies must allocate large sums of money for conducting such programs. Superintendents must be given blocks of time, from several weeks to several months, free from the routine chores in order to refresh and renew periodically their professional perspectives and skills. School districts must be prepared to share part of the costs, since they will be one of the primary beneficiaries of such a program.

If the research on educational change be valid, the educational leader is the key to the introduction of change in the schools. The most important device, then, for accomplishing change is the preparation of administrators to perform their responsibilities as leaders in changing institutions. *It is imperative now that USOE mount programs of in-service education for administrators, that it provide funds for other agencies to conduct in-service programs and that it otherwise assist in providing the means through which adequate programs of in-service education can be mounted.*

It is further evident that the in-service education of administrators must be continuous and that it must reach out as closely as possible to the locales in which administrators are situated. Effective in-service education must, to a greater extent, be brought into the field so that superintendents are not always expected to come to campus or other training centers.

It is apparent that such a pattern will involve the participation of more than the staffs of colleges and universities. Where feasible state departments of education and state administrators' associations should also be involved. *Since it has already established the linkages among the various agencies dealing with educational administration, UCEA could well be the spearhead for coordinating efforts and developing the conceptual framework through which quality programs could be initiated.*

(3) *New Organizational Models.* The organizational models for structuring the school organization which are available to the superintendent do not provide solutions to the most critical problems which confront the schools today. Changes are taking place not only in society but also in the nature of the school organization and the characteristics of the people who are professionally employed in it. An urbanized community makes different demands upon the authority structure of the schools than does the rural village. Leadership roles in public schools today cannot realistically be restructured on the basis of an organizational model which is strictly hierarchial. It is essential that efforts be expended to analyze the current research and theory of organizations so that new models of organizations relevant to the unique characteristics of educational institutions can be developed.

For much too long, the models from industry and the military have been applied to educational organizations. With the growing ability and desires of teachers to be involved in decision-making and the pressures for greater unofficial citizen involvement, these old models are rapidly becoming irrelevant and unrealistic. They are barriers rather than aids to the redefinition of roles within the school organization.

There is also a need to redefine the locus of organizational authority on a functional basis. If teachers and the public are to have specific roles in the decision-making processes, the authority inherent in each role and its relationship to the authority of the administrator must be established. The university structure has never adequately defined the parameters of collegial participation in decision-making. Because of the close scrutiny of the public over the public schools, the confused state of internal governance of higher education cannot be translated into a workable scheme for them. The task involves a great deal of creative thinking, the application of known elements of organizational research and theory, and experimentation with various devices.

(4) *The Politics of Educational Administration.* It is now perfectly clear that education is not immune from politics. It is doubtful that it ever was. At the present time, every educational agency in some form or another could be vitally affected by changing political relationships.

The character of USOE is in large part determined by order of the President and the manner in which he includes educational programs in his platform. The President could readily remove the Commissioner of Education if his policies no longer suited the particular political goals which the administration wanted to achieve. Professional concerns of the Office must frequently be subordinated to political exigencies, and Congress could accelerate or retard any of the federal programs which have been established.

State boards of education and state superintendents of public instruction are involved in politics even though, for the most part, they may be independent of the executive branch. The state superintendent must always keep on the alert to the changing temper and demands of the legislative, if not the executive branch.

On the local level, the superintendent finds it constantly more essential that he plan and coordinate with other governmental officials. Furthermore, in large eastern cities, in particular, his board members may be political appointees and his budget may be reviewed by political agencies which place educational needs in a hierarchy of total community demands for tax funds. Even if his board is elected, the local superintendent must face the voters for approval of tax levies. Not infrequently, the election of board members is a vote of confidence or rejection of the superintendent.

There is some evidence in our data to suggest that there is a dangerous dichotomy between political responsiveness and professional responsibility on all levels of educational agencies. Politics may be the art of compromise, but there are positions that frequently have to be taken upon the basis of professional knowledge and experience. Because education has become so vital in the national life as well as in the life of every community, it is difficult to maintain a professional stance when the direction of educational policy is politically useful to powerful groups.

On the other hand, education cannot live in a preserve sheltered from political involvement. It is through political instrumentalities that the resources of education are secured and that the conditions for the educational enterprise are established. Given the history of the governance of education in our society, it would be inconceivable either that all educational decisions be turned over to professional educators or that all decisions affecting education and the resources it consumes would be allocated to a single level of government. Educational decisions will be made by both professional educators and elected or appointed officials, and various types of decisions will continue to be made on local, state, and national levels.

Several basic issues are involved. They arise from the fact that no consistent rationale has been established in regard to the relationships of various political units to the educational enterprise. Confusion exists regarding the proper role and the limitations which are desirable on each level, and the superintendent of schools is frequently the individual within the local school district who must work among all the inter-relationships without guidelines specific enough to assure him that he is operating within bounds and in the best interests of the educational function. He is frequently vulnerable to attack for his inconsistency, but he has little if any help in formulating a consistent pattern of relationships.

Two particular facets of the superintendent's political involvement need clarification. First, many studies are needed to understand the problems of the political involvement of the superintendent within the local community and the consequences for the public schools of different patterns of involvement. Second, some clear formulation needs to be made of the desirable patterns of relationships which should exist among the various levels of government concerned with education. Confusion and controversy now exist, and the result is that patterns are established as power over education is usurped by one agency or another.

The issues involved in political control over education are clearly controversial, and it is doubtful that a concensus will ever be achieved. Both educators and the public, however, need clearly established standards by which the effect of decisions made on various levels can be evaluated.

(5) *Specific Problem Areas.* Each of the problem areas listed in Chapter II and discussed at the beginning of this chapter suggests a range of concerns for all educational agencies. Most of these problems will be with us in one form or another for a long time. Typically, in the field of educational administration, every problem has to be met *de novo* because we have no instrumentalities for recording professional experiences for dealing with them.

Each of the problem areas, and possibly others that may be identified, should be carefully and systematically studied. USOE should provide funds for both basic research and development, in order to obtain the essential knowledge needed about these problem areas and techniques for dealing effectively with them. We need to know how superintendents have identified and analyzed their problems, what strategies they have employed, and what success they have had. We need to know the consequences that ensue from different policies, and under what conditions various strategies either succeed or fail. Analysts from various disciplines might well be engaged to review the experiences, the conditions under which the experiences take place, and the consequences that are associated with them. Specialists in educational administration might work with such analysts to develop technologies for administrators to use with confidence when confronted with such problems.

USOE could well devise a means for establishing a network among institutions throughout the country whereby data about these problems would be collected, stored, and periodically analyzed in order to establish a record of the experience of the practitioners in the field. Such information would add immeasurably to the wealth of data upon which the basic researchers could further embark and through which the content of preparatory programs could be revised and kept up to date.

(6) *The Role of Education in Sub-cultures of American Society.* Some of the frustrations of superintendents appear to arise out of the fact that the educational profession really doesn't know how relevant education is to vast segments of our society. Educators still have the image of educational motivations that arise out of a particular set of aspirations and value orientations, and little is known about the motivations in school for children who come from many of the sub-cultures of our society. Before education can become relevant to these children *educators need to know more about the sub-cultures and how their value patterns can fit into the culture of the school.*

As it is, the culture of the school is fairly restrictive. Readiness to participate in that sub-culture is dependent upon its relevance to the individual child and his discovery of congruence between the rewards which it offers, the aspirations which he has, and the possibility of his attaining those goals through the instrumentality of the schools. For many children and youth in our society, this congruence has been lacking. There is a need for considerable research and experimentation so that educators can learn the techniques of applying their old adage to these children; namely, "Start where the learner is!"

(7) *Education and Critical Social Issues.* Administrators are well aware that the schools are called upon to serve social and political needs as well as exclusively educational ends. They resist going beyond the educational functions even though they recognize that the schools are a primary institution through which social and political objectives can be achieved. One reason for their reluctance is that they recognize that political objectives frequently require the subordination of what they

call educational functions to pressing social needs. This strategy runs counter to the socialization of the administrator who has been trained to think of education as a priority area in itself. He has been sensitized to what happens to children when they are pawns for the accomplishment of other people's purposes.

A second factor is that the administrator is not trained to lead in this realm of activity. He conceives of himself as a manager of a narrow educational enterprise and not as a social engineer. He is uncomfortable in the latter role because he sees that it involves him more deeply in politics. Because of the heterogeneous values in the community he recognizes how controversial and tensionful such a role might be. On the other hand, he recognizes that social objectives may not be capable of achievement except through the involvement of the schools.

The consequences of the use of the schools as agencies for resolving social issues and achieving political objectives should be carefully and extensively studied. What happens to the schools when they become instrumentalities for eliminating discrimination? For relieving the problems of segregation? For reducing the ill-effects of economic disadvantage? For remedying the problems of mental illness? For replacing the functions of other social agencies when they fail? Schoolmen are reluctant to become involved because they see no end to this involvement, and they see the corruption of the educational function that has taken place when, in less fortunate countries, the school has become a primary tool for the achievement of the political ends of the particular party or group in power.

The superintendent's concern seems to arise from a fear that the schools are engaged in an aimless cultural drift, still accreting functions that are imposed upon it without analyzing how these relate to the fundamental objectives of education or in what way they might contaminate the principal role of the school in a democratic society.

Before society allows the schools to drift too far, it should give educational leaders some assistance by answering their concerns about social involvement and establishing a consistent philosophy that enables them either to incorporate such activities within the legitimated functions of the schools or to have a firm basis for resisting and rejecting their being so used.

(8) *Forecasting Future Problems.* Superintendents frequently complain that the schools seem to flit from crisis to crisis. They never seem to get ahead of their problems, which are upon them before they have

had any forewarning. They asked if there is a way or an instrumentality through which problems could be forecast so that appropriate points of attack could be developed before they become critical. *Some official body, such as USOE, should establish a means through which a continuous projection of educational needs and issues can be made and both corrective and preventive strategies can be established. A major function of the Regional Offices of USOE in cooperation with the National Center for Educational Information might well be to maintain close communication with state departments of education and school districts to identify local and regional trends and their implications for the development of appropriate federal legislation.*

(9) *Evaluations of Proposals for Change and New Products.* Closely associated with several of the factors above, *it would be advantageous to superintendents for some agency to make careful assessments of the educational advantages of proposed changes and innovations in education while they are in the process of development and before they are generally introduced.* As previously indicated, superintendents feel that educators are guilty of bandwagonitis. They jump into programs not yet carefully evaluated in order to keep up with their neighbors and to avoid being caught as laggards. The result is that they engage in many enterprises that have low potential for success and that give no promise of being any better than the old methods they were designed to replace.

Perhaps it would be dangerous to give this type of power to a single agency which could then control the future destinies of education throughout the country. Superintendents might well object to this procedure as they have objected to proposals for the establishment of national programs for educational assessment. The minimum that might be desirable is the establishment of some criteria as the basis for evaluations of materials and programs.

The technology of education has now become a major economic asset for private enterprise. To the extent that they are developing means through which instruction within the schools can be improved and facilitated, they are rendering desirable service and deserve to profit. On the other hand, it is possible that through questionable practices some agencies will promote devices, plans, and programs surrounded by an aura of research and respectability beyond that which is merited. They will, in effect, prey upon the public purse and take advantage of the lack of resources within education for adequate product evaluation. Just as certification is imposed for the purpose of protecting the public against the malpractice of sub-qualified personnel, so the establishment of standards for the evaluation of products would be a device for protecting the public against the exploitation of its treasury by unethical businesses or manufacturing processes.

(10) *Professional Associations for Administrators.* Noticeably lacking in this analysis is a chapter on professional associations for the superintendent. One reason is that there has been little to report from the data which were collected. No detailed programs exist among the state associations to assist administrators in formulating strategies on the vital problems affecting them. Superintendents do not expect such aid from their associations. Traditional types of meetings are held. Speakers present both inspirational and professional speeches. Superintendents engage in "bull sessions," and state departments of education present reports on legislation and housekeeping chores. Superintendents consider their state associations to be socially enjoyable but not appreciably effective in representing or assisting them. In most instances, they have legislative programs, but relatively few associations have full-time executives, and no concentrated programs are developed. Traditionally, the suprintendents have worked through teachers' associations. However, there is dissension within their ranks about forming their own independent organizations.

Their national association does not differ greatly. The AASA concentrates a great deal of its resources and attention upon its annual national convention. It sponsors some work of national committees on issues of major importance to education, and its publications are considered helpful by most superintendents. The superintendents think well of their national association, but they do not expect much from it. They feel it is a captive of NEA. One superintendent expressed a common attitude when he said that its statement on collective negotiations was "just a bowlful of soft soap!" Others hoped that it could separate from NEA because they feared it could never be of assistance to them as long as it was so situated that NEA could dominate its policies and perspectives. Several indicated that they find it embarrassing to belong to AASA so long as it is a department of NEA, whose local affiliates are aggressively negotiating with their school boards. Others feel that the presence of AASA in NEA helps maintain balance in its program and prevents a dangerous fragmentation of the educational profession.

If the AASA has a program for in-service education, it affects only a few administrators. Most of them feel remote from its operations and lack contact with its functionaries. They do feel that AASA has been of some assistance on national legislation. They would want it to do more.

The present status of the superintendent in the educational profession calls for a re-evaluation of his professional memberships and the role of the specific organizations which exist for his purposes. Since there is only a handful of superintendents in any state, compared to the number of teachers, their association can never have the financial resources of the teachers' associations. There might be considerable difficulty in attempting to coordinate or combine the administrators' associations with the school board associations, since some differences are bound to exist, and the administrator needs that association which can render specific assistance in times of crisis.

Regardless of these problems, the superintendent needs the same types of assistance from his associations which teachers receive from theirs. Both national and state associations need to devise means to vitalize their conferences and conventions and engage in cooperation with other agencies in in-service education programs. Professional associations should study their publications programs to determine how they can help to disseminate current knowledge to their membership. Until they reformulate their roles, the professional associations cannot render the services which superintendents need.

(11) *University Council for Educational Administration.* UCEA is an agency which relates to professors of educational administration rather than to superintendents. It is within our purview since what it does affects the preparation of administrators. In the few years of its existence it has made considerable impact upon universities and individual professors. It can play a major role in the improvement of preparatory programs and in the development of adequate in-service education programs for both superintendents and professors of educational administration. It has already been operating with this latter group.

Its difficulties stem from the fact that it is a confederation and its work must be implemented through the universities which it serves. There does not appear to be a sufficient emphasis among its membership for implementing its recommendations or incorporating all professors of educational administration in its activities. It is scarcely visible to superintendents. Its standards are justifiably high, but, as a consequence, it relates almost exclusively to the major preparatory institutions, and only indirectly through the use of its publications do non-member institutions benefit from its developmental and research activities.

UCEA has dynamic leadership and can marshal for its programs the most competent administrators and professors in the country, as well as from other English-speaking countries. Perhaps its emphasis has been too heavy upon research, theory, and the conceptual tasks and insufficient upon the human relations, the political, and the technical tasks of the superintendent. It has promise for becoming an increasingly effective agency, but colleges and universities should consider how its efforts can be used to greater advantage internally.

(12) *State Departments of Education.* Much has already been said about state departments of education. Their needs and the opportunities for their achieving greater effectiveness have been well presented by R. L. Johns and Roald Campbell,[2] and we will not reiterate their recommendations or those presented in Chapter 4 at this point. Suffice it to say, that state departments have a major responsibility for improving their effectiveness and that USOE has a major responsibility in helping them achieve greater stature.

(13) *The United States Office of Education.* Many implications and recommendations for the role of USOE have been made throughout this report. We will not summarize them here, but a few final points seem to be pertinent.

First, when USOE became a large funding agency, the role of the specialist in educational administration all but disappeared. The Office was left with no department which was particularly charged with the responsibility for maintaining current knowledge useful specifically to educational administrators. It was also left with no department which, through scholarship and close association with the field, could project the needs and future problems for school organization and administration. Within the current structure of education, USOE must deal with the problems of administrators. It cannot deal directly with teachers since federal programs have first to be implemented through administrative channels. *It would appear to be vital both to the successful operation of federal programs and to the improvement of administration throughout the country that a department of educational organization and administration be established.* We are not sure what form it should

---

2 R. L. Johns. "State Organization and Responsibilities for Education," in Edgar L. Morphet and Charles O. Ryan (Eds.), *Implications for Education of Prospective Changes in Society.* (Denver: Designing Education for the Future, 1967), pp. 248-266.
Roald F. Campbell. "Supplementary Statement." *Ibid.*, pp. 267-272.

take, but we are sure that administrators feel the loss of the specialists and that USOE would find their reestablishment advantageous in fulfilling its responsibilities. The leadership role of USOE implies more than the distribution of federal funds. It is that agency which can effectively represent both the public and the profession in charting the course of education in the future. In this sense it can be the agency which provides both direction and mediation for the different interests that relate to education.

Second, Congress has not been consistent in the establishment of the structures through which federal programs are administered. Some educational programs operate through state departments of education; some directly involve school districts, although the state departments play some role; some operate through agencies other than USOE and do not have the experience of USOE in working within the educational arena. *To establish better relations with the field, USOE should set up the same format, structure, and policies on all federal programs. All federal programs with which the public schools are involved should be channeled through USOE.* Much of the confusion could be eliminated in this way, and better working relationships with public school officials could be established.

Third, USOE cannot be a professionally responsible agency so long as it is submerged under political pressures and has to be responsive to political agencies. Obviously, it cannot be removed from politics, but it cannot serve its educational functions adequately if its professional integrity must constantly be submerged to political exigencies. The issues involved must be faced and analyzed, and its future course in both government and education must be charted. Inevitably, the federal government will play an increasing role in education, and USOE will be the instrumentality through which federal programs are implemented. *It is in the interests of education and the public it serves that its role be clearly defined.*

In Retrospect

In retrospect, the authors feel like the fabled ruler who sent out his emissaries to discover the evils which existed within his kingdom. They returned telling him that evil abounded throughout the realm. This study has not been an evaluation of educational administration. It did not seek to define all of the areas of successful and effective operations of the superintendency. There would be much to report had it done so.

Considering all of the problems faced by public education, the social currents affecting the transitional role of the schools, and the manner in which the schools have been serving the American public, one must acknowledge the massive accomplishments of superintendents in directing and improving educational programs through troubled times.

Expectations for education are high, and the need for greater adaptability and quality is more pressing. It is because of these factors that we justify our limited and skewed perception of the field. It was because of their concern for the future well-being of education that superintendents participated so willingly and so forthrightly in our study.

As it has in the past, the superintendency today and in the future points the direction for the educational enterprise. To the extent that this position of leadership within the framework of the school organization can be made more effective, the schools will be improved and the needs of our society well served.

Appendixes

Participants in the Study

	Superintendents	College and University Personnel	State Department of Education Personnel	Regional Educational Laboratory Personnel
San Francisco Area	9	6	2	2
Oklahoma City Area	9	6	2	1
Chicago Area	11	9	2	1
New York Area	9	9	3	2
Atlanta Area	8	4	2	1
Totals	46	34	11	7

Participants in Formal Study Conference Areas	98
American Association of School Administrators	2
USOE Personnel	27
Office of Economic Opportunity	1
Total	128
Additional Superintendents in Informal Studies	37
Additional University and Other Personnel	15
Total	180

APPENDIX B

B-1

Interview with Participating Superintendents

1. What problems were discussed at the conference which you feel are particularly relevant to this and neighboring school districts?

1.1 In what specific ways do these problems become manifest here?

1.2 What are the primary causes for these problems?

1.3 What do you see locally as the important barriers to their solution and the factors which have to be resolved before they can be solved?

1.4 What are the main sources from which you can obtain assistance in developing approaches to these problems?

1.5 What resources do you have in your own school district for assisting you in developing strategies for dealing with these problems?

1.6 In the long range, which of these problems are most significant to you?

2. What additional problems do you feel should be noted?

   (Same questions as under 1)

3. In what ways are the following professional agencies helpful to local school districts in developing approaches to these and other problems which might arise? (Probe on how they might be more helpful) (Probe on preparatory, in-service education for administrators, research and consultative services for starred items.)

   *3.1 State Departments of Education

   *3.2 State administrators' associations

   *3.3 National administrators' associations

   3.4 Local, state and national teachers' associations (NEA and AFT)

   *3.5 Colleges and universities in your area

   3.6 National and state school boards' associations

   *3.7 U. S. Office of Education

   3.8 Office of Economic Opportunity

   3.9 Regional educational laboratories

   3.10 Other agencies

4. What new problems confronting education do you see emerging within the next five years?

   4.1 What programs would you particularly suggest of various agencies for developing resources to assist administrators to deal with these problems?

B-2

Interview with State Department of Education Personnel

1. How general and significant are the problems which were raised at the conference?

    1.1 How are these problems specifically manifested in the state?
    1.2 What are the primary causes for these problems?
    1.3 What do you see as the most significant barriers to their solution and the factors which have to be resolved before they can be solved?
    1.4 What promising approaches are emerging in the state for dealing with these problems?

2. What additional problems do you feel should be noted?

    (Same questions as under 1)

3. How does your State Department of Education help to identify significant problems facing administrators?

    3.1 What systematic programs are employed?

4. What programs does your State Department of Education provide for helping administrators develop approaches to their problems?

    4.1 Research
    4.2 Conferences and workshops
    4.3 In-service education
    4.4 Consultation services
    4.5 Grants to districts

5. What do you see as the ways in which the following agencies are helpful to local school districts in developing approaches to these and other problems which may arise? (Probe starred items for preparatory, in-service education for administrators, research, and consultative services.)

    *5.1 State Departments of Education
    *5.2 State administrators' associations
    *5.3 National administrators' associations
    5.4 Local, state and national teachers' associations (NEA and AFT)
    *5.5 Colleges and universities in your area
    5.6 National and state school boards' associations
    *5.7 U. S. Office of Education
    5.8 Office of Economic Opportunity
    5.9 Regional educational laboratories
    5.10 Other agencies

6. What new problems confronting education do you see emerging in the next five years?

    6.1 What programs would you particularly suggest of various agencies for developing resources to assist administrators to deal with these problems?

B-3

Interview with University Personnel

1. What are the primary characteristics of your programs in administration, including pre-service, in-service, and research?

   1.1 What emphasis or balance do you maintain among the various programs?

2. In what ways does your staff maintain contact with administrators in the field?

3. What types of assistance in developing approaches to superintendents' problems do you offer presently employed administrators?

   3.1 In-service training programs

   3.2 Conferences and workshops

   3.3 School surveys and special studies

   3.4 Resource and consultant services

   3.5 Other

   3.6 How adequate do you consider each of the above programs to be for helping administrators in your area with their problems?

4. Do you maintain any systematic programs for identifying major problems confronting school administrators? If so, please describe.

   4.1 What devices do you employ for reflecting findings about problems of administrators in your pre-service, in-service, and research programs?

5. Do you have a bureau of field services? What are the activities in which it is engaged?

6. What changes in your administrative preparation programs are contemplated?

   6.1 Do you work with any other agencies outside of the university or college in the evaluation, alteration and development of your programs?

      6.1.1 Pre-service

      6.1.2 In-service

      6.1.3 Research

7. How is your program related to any of the following agencies?

   7.1 State Departments of Education

   7.2 State and national administrators' associations

   7.3 Local, state and national teachers' associations

   7.4 Associations or consortiums of colleges and universities

   7.5 State and national school boards' associations

   7.6 U. S. Office of Education

   7.7 Social sciences divisions of the university

   7.8 Other academic divisions of the university

   7.9 Office of Economic Opportunity

   7.10 Regional educational laboratories

   7.11 Other agencies

8. What are the major ways in which the State Department of Education in this state assist school administrators?

8.1 How adequate are its services to school administrators?

8.2 What problems does it have in relating to the needs of school administrators?

8.3 How do you think it could best discharge its responsibilities to school administrators?

9. What are the major ways in which the U. S. Office of Education works with school administrators in this state?

(Same questions as in 8)

10. What new problems confronting education do you see emerging in the next five years?

10.1 What programs would you particularly suggest of various agencies for developing resources to assist administrators to deal with this problem?

B-4

Interview with Regional Educational Laboratory Personnel

1. What is the content and scope of the program which the laboratory intends to conduct in this region?
Probe: Describe activities

2. How does the regional laboratory intend to identify significant problems facing administrators?

3. What programs (does) (will) the laboratory provide for helping administrators develop approaches to their problems?

3.1 Research
3.2 Conferences and workshops
3.3 In-service education
3.4 Consultation services
3.5 Financial assistance

4. What are some of the significant barriers to the development of programs relating to school administration?

5. What new problems confronting education do you see as emerging within the next five years?